The Ultimate Retirement Bucket List

150 Hilarious and Unexpected Adventures, Activities and Discoveries to Fill Your Golden Years

Garry Wanderwell

Contents

Copyright

The Ultimate Retirement Bucket List: 150 Hilarious and Unexpected Adventures, Activities and Discoveries to Fill Your Golden Years

Copyright © 2023 by Garry Wanderwell

All rights reserved.

No portion of this book may be reproduced in any form without written permission from the publisher or author, except as permitted by U.S. copyright law.

Introduction

Welcome to "The Ultimate Retirement Bucket List: 150 Hilarious and Unexpected Adventures, Activities and Discoveries to Fill Your Golden Years"! The moment you've been working toward is finally here – retirement! It's time to kick back, relax, and seize the opportunity to make the most of your newfound freedom.

This book is your essential guide to transform your retirement years into a thrilling journey of exploration and self-discovery. It doesn't matter whether you're an adrenaline junkie, a cultural aficionado, or a nature enthusiast; there's something for everyone in these pages. From the absurd to the enlightening, we've compiled a diverse array of activities that will not only make you laugh but also leave you feeling accomplished and alive.

We've designed this book to help you embrace the spirit of adventure and break away from the monotony of routine, all while fostering meaningful connections with the people and world around you. Every experience shared in this book is a stepping stone towards crafting your own unique and unforgettable retirement story.

So, let's dive in! Your golden years await, filled with laughter, excitement, and unforgettable memories. It's time to write the next chapter of your life, and make it the most thrilling one yet!

Category I: Let the Fun Begin

Bucket List # 1

Laughter Yoga: Stretch, Laugh, and Connect

"Laughter is the best Medicine, and Yoga is the Music of the Body. Together, they Create a Symphony of Joy." – Anonymous –

Imagine combining the therapeutic power of laughter with the rejuvenating energy of yoga. Welcome to the world of Laughter Yoga, a delightful activity that can transform your retirement years into a time of fun, connection, and vitality. Laughter Yoga is a unique practice that brings together people from all walks of life to share in the joy of laughter, deep breathing, and simple yoga exercises.

Laughter Yoga is not only an entertaining way to spend your time but also has numerous health benefits. It helps to reduce stress, strengthen the immune system, and promote a positive mindset. By participating in Laughter Yoga sessions, you'll find yourself feeling more energetic, happy, and rejuvenated.

Getting started is easy. Look for local Laughter Yoga clubs or classes in your area, or connect with others online through social media groups and video sessions. You can even start your own group with friends and family. The best part is that you don't need any prior experience in yoga or a sense of humor to enjoy the benefits.

Remember, age is just a number, and the joy of laughter is timeless. Embrace the art of Laughter Yoga and make your golden years sparkle with happiness and newfound connections.

Laughter Yoga is like a garden of joy, where each giggle is a seed, each deep breath is a sunbeam, and each connection is a flower in full bloom. Together, you'll create a beautiful, ever-growing oasis of happiness that will sustain you through the best years of your life.

In the end, Laughter Yoga is like a key that unlocks the door to a treasure chest of happiness. As you embrace this practice, you'll find your days filled with joy, laughter, and connection. Your golden years will be more than just a time of rest and relaxation; they'll be a celebration of life itself, full of unexpected adventures and delightful discoveries.

Bucket List # 2

Flash Mobbing: Dance Your Way to Happiness

"Dance Like Nobody's Watching, because in a Flash Mob, everyone is Dancing with you."

– Anonymous –

Picture yourself grooving to the beat of your favorite song, surrounded by a sea of smiling faces, all dancing in unison. Welcome to the world of flash mobbing, a delightful adventure that combines dance, surprise, and togetherness to create unforgettable moments of happiness. By participating in flash mobs, you'll add a thrilling twist to your golden years and dance your way to happiness.

Flash mobbing is an excellent way for retirees to stay active, make new friends, and explore their creative side. It's an opportunity to learn new dance moves, feel the rhythm of the music, and express yourself freely.

Getting started is simple. Search for local flash mob events, dance classes, or social media groups that organize flash mobs in your area. Many events are open to beginners, so you don't need any prior dance experience. All you need is a positive attitude and a willingness to have a great time.

Remember, your golden years are meant to be filled with fun and adventure. Flash mobbing is the perfect way to infuse your days with excitement and create lasting memories.

Think of flash mobbing as a delightful surprise party, where every dancer is both the guest of honor and the life of the party. As you join hands and dance together, you'll create a beautiful tapestry of movement and joy that will energize and inspire you throughout the best years of your life.

In addition to the physical benefits of dancing, flash mobbing offers a unique opportunity for personal growth. As you learn to trust your instincts and express yourself through movement, you'll develop greater self-confidence and a deeper appreciation for life's spontaneity. Embrace the world of flash mobbing with open arms and an open heart, and you'll find that happiness is just a dance step away.

Bucket List # 3

Spontaneous Road Trips: Hit the Open Road

"Life is a Journey, not a Destination, and the Open Road is where you'll find your Greatest Adventures." – Unknown –

There's something magical about hitting the open road with no set plan, just the spirit of adventure guiding you. Spontaneous road trips offer a thrilling opportunity to explore the unknown, make unforgettable memories, and rediscover the joy of living in the moment. Your golden years are the perfect time to embrace the freedom of the open road and let it led you to new experiences.

Spontaneous road trips are important for retirees because they allow you to break free from routines and explore your surroundings with fresh eyes. It's a chance to reconnect with your sense of wonder, forge new friendships, and create lasting memories along the way.

Getting started is as easy as grabbing a map, hopping in your car, and letting your instincts guide you. Choose a direction, and let the road reveal its secrets to you. You can visit quaint towns, breath-taking national parks, or unique roadside attractions. The beauty of spontaneous road trips is that there's no right or wrong way to do it – the adventure is all yours to create.

Spontaneous road trips are like a treasure hunt, where each turn of the road reveals a hidden gem, waiting to be discovered. As you journey through your golden years, let the open road be your guide, leading you to a wealth of laughter, adventure, and joy that will fill your heart and soul with memories to last a lifetime.

Road trips are like a vibrant painting, where each destination is a brushstroke, and the open road is your canvas. As you explore the world around you, you'll create a beautiful masterpiece of memories, laughter, and adventure that will be a testament to the joy and freedom of your golden years. So, buckle up and let the open road be your guide to a world of endless possibilities.

Bucket List # 4

Geocaching: A High-Tech Treasure Hunt

"Adventure is out there, waiting to be Discovered, and Geocaching is the key to Unlocking its Hidden Treasures." – Unknown –

Imagine embarking on a thrilling treasure hunt that combines the great outdoors with cutting-edge technology. Welcome to the world of geocaching, a modern-day adventure that invites you to explore your surroundings, solve puzzles, and discover hidden treasures. Your golden years are the perfect time to embrace this exciting hobby and let your inner explorer come to life.

Geocaching is important for retirees because it encourages you to stay active, both mentally and physically. It's a fun way to connect with nature, exercise your problem-solving skills, and meet fellow adventurers along the way.

Getting started is simple. All you need is a smartphone or GPS device, and a sense of adventure. Visit the official geocaching website or download a geocaching app to access a treasure trove of hidden caches in your area. Follow the coordinates and clues provided to locate the hidden containers, which can range from tiny capsules to large boxes. Inside, you'll find a logbook to sign and sometimes even small trinkets to exchange.

Remember, these are the best years of your life, and geocaching offers a unique opportunity to fill your days with fun, excitement, and a sense of discovery.

Geocaching is like an interactive storybook, where each hidden cache is a chapter waiting to be unveiled. As you journey through your golden years, let geocaching guide you on a thrilling adventure that will keep your mind sharp, your heart full, and your spirit forever young like a hidden treasure map that spans the entire globe, with each cache representing a secret corner of the world waiting to be discovered. As you journey through your golden years, let geocaching guide you on a thrilling adventure that will fill your heart with joy, your mind with wonder, and your life with unforgettable memories.

Bucket List # 5

Paint and Sip Classes: Unleash Your Inner Artist

"Creativity takes Courage, but with each Brushstroke, you'll Discover the Masterpiece that Lies Within." – Unknown –

Paint and sip classes are a delightful way to tap into your creative side while enjoying the company of others in a relaxed, fun atmosphere. These classes invite you to explore your artistic talents, laugh with friends, and indulge in a glass of your favorite beverage, all while creating a beautiful work of art. Embracing your inner artist during your golden years is a wonderful way to fill your days with color, joy, and self-expression.

Paint and sip classes are important for retirees because they offer a unique opportunity to learn new skills, cultivate your creativity, and build connections with fellow art enthusiasts. These classes can help you unwind, boost your self-esteem, and create lasting memories as you journey through your golden years.

Getting started is as simple as searching for paint and sip classes in your local area. Many studios offer beginner-friendly sessions that cater to all skill levels, so you can feel confident and supported as you embark on your artistic journey. All you need is an open mind, a willingness to try something new, and a sense of humor as you laugh and learn together with your fellow artists.

Remember, these are the best years of your life, and paint and sip classes offer a unique opportunity to explore your artistic side, connect with others, and make each day a colorful celebration.

Paint and sip classes are like a colorful bouquet of flowers, where each brushstroke adds a vibrant petal to the canvas of your life. As you explore your artistic talents during your golden years, you'll create a beautiful masterpiece of memories, laughter, and self-expression that will bring joy and color to your heart and soul. Sharing this artistic adventure with loved ones will strengthen your bonds and create cherished memories that you'll treasure for years to come.

Bucket List # 6

Dog Yoga: Stretch and Bond with Your Furry Friend

"The Best way to find Yourself is to Lose Yourself in the Service of others, especially those with Four Legs and a Wagging Tail." – Unknown –

Dog yoga, or "doga," is a delightful fusion of yoga and bonding with your furry friend. It offers a unique opportunity to enhance your physical and mental well-being while deepening the connection with your beloved pet. In your golden years, dog yoga provides a chance to discover new ways to stay active, healthy, and engaged, all while enjoying the company of your loyal companion.

Doga is important for retirees because it promotes relaxation, flexibility, and mindfulness. It also helps strengthen the bond between you and your dog, resulting in a more harmonious and joyful relationship.

Getting started with dog yoga is simple. Look for local yoga studios or instructors offering doga classes, or search online for instructional videos and guides. Remember to consult with your veterinarian to ensure that your dog is in good health and can safely participate in doga activities. Once you're ready, grab your yoga mat, your furry friend, and an open mind, and let the magic of doga unfold.

Remember, your golden years are a time to embrace new experiences, create lasting memories, and enjoy the unconditional love of your four-legged companion.

Doga is like a dance where you and your furry friend gracefully move in harmony, creating a beautiful symphony of trust, love, and understanding. As you journey through your golden years, let dog yoga guide you on a path of health, happiness, and a deeper connection with your beloved companion. So, take a deep breath, stretch, and embrace the joy of dog yoga.

It's like a beautiful tapestry, where each pose and shared moment weaves a vibrant thread of love, trust, and understanding between you and your furry friend. As you journey through your golden years, let dog yoga guide you on a path filled with laughter, health, and a deeper connection with your beloved pet

Bucket List # 7

Dare to Karaoke: Sing Your Heart Out

"Sing like no one is Listening, Love Like you've never been hurt, Dance Like Nobody's Watching, and Live like it's Heaven on Earth." – Mark Twain –

Daring to karaoke is a fantastic way to unleash your inner superstar and fill your golden years with laughter, excitement, and unforgettable memories. Karaoke allows you to express yourself, share your favorite tunes with friends, and create joyous moments that you'll cherish for years to come.

Karaoke is important for retirees because it promotes socialization, self-expression, and the courage to step out of your comfort zone. It can also help boost your self-confidence and bring people together, fostering new friendships and deepening existing bonds.

Getting started with karaoke is as simple as finding a local karaoke bar or lounge, or even hosting a karaoke night at home. Many venues offer a wide range of songs to suit all tastes, from classic hits to modern chart-toppers. Gather your friends and family, choose your favorite tracks, and step up to the microphone with enthusiasm and confidence.

Remember, your golden years are an opportunity to embrace new experiences, laugh wholeheartedly, and celebrate life to the fullest.

Karaoke is like colorful fireworks display, where each song you sing ignites a brilliant burst of joy, laughter, and togetherness in the night sky of your golden years. As you journey through this exciting phase of life, let karaoke guide you on a path of self-expression, camaraderie, and endless fun. Your karaoke journey, you'll discover endless ways to enhance your experience and make each performance even more memorable. Consider incorporating fun themes, costumes, and friendly competitions, encouraging everyone to join in and showcase their unique talents.

To enrich your karaoke adventures is to explore different musical genres, artists, and eras. Delve into the vast world of music and challenge yourself to learn new songs, sing in different languages, or even perform duets and group numbers with friends and loved ones it's like a vibrant rainbow that arches across the sky.

Bucket List # 8

Thrift Store Fashion Show: A Budget-Friendly Style Challenge

"Fashion is about Something that Comes from Within You." – Ralph Lauren –

Thrift store fashion shows are an exciting and budget-friendly way to express your unique style, unleash your creativity, and bond with friends and family. Embrace the challenge of crafting fashionable outfits from thrifted finds, and share the fun and laughter with those closest to you.

Thrift store fashion shows are important for retirees because they promote creativity, resourcefulness, and socialization. Plus, they serve as a reminder that style and self-expression don't have to come with a hefty price tag.

To get started, gather a group of friends or family members who are up for the challenge. Plan a fun outing to your local thrift stores, and set a budget for each participant. As you shop, search for hidden gems, statement pieces, and accessories that showcase your unique style. Once everyone has their outfits, host a fashion show where you can strut your stuff, vote on your favorite looks, and celebrate your fabulous finds.

Remember, your golden years are a time to explore new adventures, create lasting memories, and celebrate your individuality.

Thrift store fashion shows are like a treasure hunt, where each unique piece you discover adds a sparkling gem to the vibrant mosaic of your golden years. As you embark on this stylish journey, let the thrill of the hunt and the joy of self-expression guide you on a path filled with laughter, connection, and unforgettable memories.

Tips to elevate your thrift store fashion adventures:

- **Theme your fashion shows:**
- **Organize a charity event**
- **Host a clothing swap.**
- **Document your fashion journey**
- **Explore different thrift store**

Thrift store fashion shows are like an artist's palette, where each carefully chosen piece adds a stroke of color and creativity to the masterpiece of your golden years. Let your unique style and flair for fashion guide you on a path filled with laughter, connection, and unforgettable memories.

Category 2: The Great Outdoors

Bucket List # 9

Hot Air Ballooning: Soar High Above the Earth

"Once you have Tasted Flight, you will Forever Walk the Earth with your Eyes Turned Skyward, for there you have been, and there you will Always Long to Return." – Leonardo da Vinci –

Hot air ballooning is a breathtaking adventure that allows you to soar high above the earth and experience the world from a whole new perspective. This exhilarating activity offers the perfect combination of excitement, tranquility, and awe-inspiring beauty, making it a must-try experience during your golden years.

Hot air ballooning is important for retirees because it encourages you to step out of your comfort zone, embrace new challenges, and create unforgettable memories. It also provides an opportunity to witness the beauty of nature from a unique vantage point, sparking a deeper appreciation for the world around you.

Getting started with hot air ballooning is as simple as finding a reputable ballooning company near you. Many companies offer group flights or private experiences, so you can share this amazing adventure with friends, family, or your significant other. Make sure to book your flight in advance, as weather conditions can affect availability.

Remember, your golden years are an opportunity to explore new horizons, conquer your fears, and create memories that will last a lifetime.

Hot air ballooning is like a magnificent eagle soaring through the sky of your golden years, each breathtaking view adding a brush-stroke of wonder and awe to the canvas of your life. As you embark on this exhilarating journey, let the thrill of flight guide you on a path filled with adventure, beauty, and unforgettable moments.

Tips and ideas to make each flight an even more memorable experience:

- **Capture the moment**
- **Celebrate special occasions**
- **Travel and explore**
- **Learn more about ballooning**
- **Share your experience**

Hot air ballooning is like a colorful kite dancing gracefully in the wind of your golden years, each gust lifting you higher and revealing new wonders to explore. Let the magic of flight guide you on a path filled with adventure, excitement, and awe-inspiring beauty.

Bucket List # 10

Ziplining: Fly Through the Trees

"Life is Either a Daring Adventure or Nothing at All." – Helen Keller –

Ziplining is an exhilarating activity that lets you fly through the trees, feeling the wind on your face as you glide from platform to platform. It's an exciting way to reconnect with nature, challenge yourself, and create unforgettable memories during your golden years.

Ziplining is important for retirees because it encourages you to embrace new experiences, conquer your fears, and bond with others who share your sense of adventure. It also provides an opportunity to appreciate the beauty of nature from a thrilling vantage point, igniting a newfound passion for the great outdoors.

To get started with ziplining, research reputable zipline tour operators in your area or at your next travel destination. Most operators offer a variety of courses to suit different skill levels, ensuring a fun and safe experience for everyone. Before booking, make sure to check their safety standards, certifications, and customer reviews.

Remember, your golden years are a time to explore new heights, overcome challenges, and create memories that will last a lifetime.

Ziplining is like a powerful gust of wind carrying you through the treetops of your golden years, each exhilarating ride adding a burst of excitement and joy to your journey. As you embark on this thrilling adventure, let the spirit of the wind guide you on a path filled with laughter, connection, and unforgettable moments.

Tips and ideas to enhance each experience and make it even more memorable:

- **Embrace the challenge**
- **Share the adventure**
- **Document your journey**
- **Explore new locations**
- **Learn and grow**

Ziplining is like a vibrant hummingbird darting through the colorful foliage of your golden years, each thrilling swoop and glide adding a spark of excitement and wonder to your journey. As you embark on this heart-pounding adventure, let the spirit of the hummingbird guide you on a path filled with exhilaration, growth, and unforgettable moments.

Bucket List # 11

Whale Watching: Encounter Majestic Marine Life

"In Every Walk with Nature, one Receives Far more than he Seeks." –John Muir –

Whale watching is a breathtaking activity that offers a chance to witness the beauty and majesty of some of the largest creatures on our planet. It's a unique opportunity to connect with nature, learn about marine life, and create unforgettable memories during your golden years.

Whale watching is important for retirees because it encourages a sense of wonder and appreciation for the natural world. It also provides an opportunity to learn about the ocean's ecosystem and the fascinating creatures that inhabit it. Moreover, it allows you to share this memorable experience with loved ones or newfound friends.

To get started with whale watching, research reputable whale watching tour operators in your area or at your next coastal travel destination. Most operators offer guided tours led by knowledgeable experts who can teach you about the whales and their behaviors. Before booking, check the tour operator's safety standards, certifications, and customer reviews to ensure a safe and enjoyable experience.

Whale watching is like an enchanting symphony playing in the deep blue sea of your golden years, each mesmerizing encounter with these majestic creatures adding a note of awe and inspiration to your journey. As you embark on this captivating adventure, let the spirit of the whales guide you on a path filled with curiosity, connection, and unforgettable moments.

Consider the following tips to enhance your adventures:

- **Keep learning**
- **Share your passion**
- **Embrace the unexpected**
- **Document your journey**
- **Pay it forward**

Your golden years are like a vast ocean filled with wonder and possibilities. Whale watching is just one of the many ways to dive into this ocean and swim alongside the magnificent creatures that inhabit it. Explore, and let the waves of life carry you to new and uncharted depths of discovery and joy.

Bucket List # 12

River Rafting: Conquer the Rapids

"Life is Either a Daring adventure or Nothing at All." – Helen Keller –

River rafting is an exhilarating and unforgettable experience that allows you to conquer the rapids and rediscover the thrill of adventure during your golden years. It's an opportunity to test your limits, bond with your fellow rafters, and reconnect with the power and beauty of nature.

River rafting is important for retirees because it helps you break away from your routine and challenge yourself in a whole new way. It provides an adrenaline rush that reignites your sense of adventure and reminds you that age is just a number. Plus, river rafting is a fantastic way to build camaraderie with friends, family, or other like-minded retirees as you work together to navigate the rapids.

Remember, your golden years are an opportunity to embrace the river of life and all its twists and turns. Dive into new adventures and let the current carry you to exciting, uncharted territories.

In your golden years is like dancing with the wild rhythm of life. You'll find that the powerful waves of adventure propel you forward, washing away any doubts and fears, and leaving you with a newfound sense of strength and vitality.

It's important to keep pushing your boundaries and exploring your potential. River rafting is just one of the many exciting adventures that can help you do just that. As you ride the rapids and conquer the challenges that come your way, you'll discover a newfound sense of confidence and accomplishment.

Tip to consider the following enhance your experience:

- **Take a course**
- **Join a club**
- **Explore new rivers**
- **Give back**

As you continue to embrace the exciting world of river rafting, remember that life, like the river, is full of twists, turns, and surprises. Embrace the journey and let the rapids of adventure carry you to the farthest reaches of your potential. After all, your golden years are a time to celebrate the limitless possibilities that life has to offer.

Bucket List # 13

Birdwatching: Discover the Beauty of Feathered Friends

"Life is not Measured by the Number of Breaths we take, but by the Moments that take our Breath Away." – Maya Angelou –

Birdwatching: Discover the Beauty of Feathered Friends

The wonder of the natural world is just outside your door, and bird-watching is the perfect way to embrace it! Imagine walking through a peaceful forest, your ears catching the sweet melodies of birds singing, your eyes feasting on the vibrant colors of their feathers. As you embark on your birdwatching journey, you'll not only fill your heart with joy but also experience a newfound sense of adventure.

Birdwatching is not just about spotting our feathered friends; it's about discovering the diverse world they live in and learning to appreciate their unique beauty. The thrill of identifying a new species or observing their fascinating behaviors can provide endless excitement in your golden years.

Getting started, grab a pair of binoculars and a field guide to help you identify the birds you'll encounter. Find a local park, nature reserve, or even your backyard to begin your exploration. Finally, remember to be patient, as birds may not always make themselves visible right away. Over time, you'll develop a keen eye and become a master birder.

As you set off on this delightful adventure, you'll also find that bird-watching is a brilliant way to connect with fellow enthusiasts. Joining birdwatching clubs or participating in group outings will not only enrich your experiences but also create lasting friendships.

In conclusion, birdwatching is like opening a window into a secret world of breathtaking beauty and remarkable creatures. It's a reminder that life is full of surprises, and your golden years are the perfect time to embrace these thrilling discoveries. So, put on your walking shoes, grab your binoculars, and let the enchanting world of birds whisk you away on a journey filled with wonder, excite-ment, and companionship.

Bucket List # 14

Glamping: Luxury Camping for the Modern Retiree

"Adventure is worthwhile." – Aesop –

Glamping: Luxury Camping for the Modern Retiree

When you think of camping, you might envision sleeping on the ground, cooking over an open fire, and battling pesky mosquitoes. But what if you could enjoy the great outdoors without sacrificing the comforts of home? Enter glamping, a perfect fusion of glamour and camping that offers the best of both worlds.

Glamping is a unique way to experience nature, combining the serenity of the outdoors with the luxury of modern amenities. Whether it's in a cozy yurt, a spacious treehouse, or a stylish airstream, glamping accommodations provide all the comforts you could want, including plush beds, private bathrooms, and even gourmet meals.

Why is glamping perfect for retirees seeking adventure? Firstly, it allows you to reconnect with nature and escape the hustle and bustle of everyday life. The fresh air, breathtaking views, and calming sounds of the wild create an atmosphere of pure relaxation and rejuvenation.

Getting started is a breeze. To plan your perfect glamping getaway, begin by researching glamping destinations that suit your preferences. From beachside retreats to mountain hideaways, there's a glamping experience for everyone. Next, book your accommodations and make a list of nearby activities you'd like to try, such as hiking, birdwatching, or stargazing.

Embarking on a glamping adventure is not only a treat for the senses but also an opportunity to make unforgettable memories with loved ones. Gather around a campfire, share stories, and bask in the simple joys of life as you enjoy this luxurious outdoor experience.

In conclusion, glamping is like taking the best parts of a five-star hotel and transplanting them into the heart of nature. It's the perfect way to embrace your golden years, indulging in comfort and adventure in equal measure. After all, these are the best years of your life, and glamping is a brilliant way to fill them with laughter, love, and unforgettable experiences.

Bucket List # 15

Stargazing: Connect with the Cosmos

"Keep your Eyes on the Stars and your Feet on the Ground." – Theodore Roosevelt –

Stargazing: Connect with the Cosmos

There's something magical about gazing up at the night sky, lost in the wonder of the twinkling stars and the vastness of the universe. Stargazing is an enchanting pastime that can bring both peace and exhilaration to your golden years, reminding you of the boundless beauty that exists beyond our small corner of the cosmos.

Stargazing is important because it can awaken your sense of wonder and curiosity. As you learn about constellations, planets, and other celestial objects, you'll find yourself connecting with the mysteries of the universe and gaining a deeper appreciation for the world around you.

Getting started with stargazing is as simple as stepping outside on a clear night and looking up. To enhance your experience, consider investing in a telescope or a pair of binoculars. A stargazing app or a star chart can also help you identify celestial bodies and track their movements across the sky.

To make the most of your stargazing experience, try heading out to a location far from city lights, where the sky is darker and the stars shine more brightly. You can even make it a social activity by inviting friends and family to join you, or attending a local stargazing event.

As you become more familiar with the night sky, you may find yourself captivated by the beauty of meteor showers, eclipses, and other celestial phenomena. These awe-inspiring events serve as a reminder of the infinite wonders that await you in your retirement.

In conclusion, stargazing is like opening a window to the universe, offering you a glimpse into the grandeur of the cosmos. Embrace this captivating hobby in your golden years and let it fill your nights with wonder, excitement, and a connection to the celestial tapestry above. After all, these are your best years ahead, and the stars are shining brightly, inviting you to join them in their cosmic dance.

Bucket List # 16

Urban Gardening: Cultivate Your Green Thumb

"The Glory of Gardening: Hands in the Dirt, head in the Sun, Heart with Nature." – Alfred Austin –

Urban Gardening: Cultivate Your Green Thumb

Even if you live in a bustling city, you can still find a way to connect with nature and enjoy the simple pleasures of gardening. Urban gardening is a delightful hobby that not only brings beauty to your surroundings but also nourishes your body and soul.

Urban gardening is important because it allows you to grow your own fresh, organic produce, beautify your living space, and create a sense of community with fellow gardeners. Additionally, tending to plants can have therapeutic benefits, reducing stress and promoting a sense of well-being.

To get started with urban gardening, all you need is a small outdoor space, such as a balcony, rooftop, or courtyard. If space is limited, consider vertical gardening or container gardening, which allow you to grow a variety of plants in a compact area.

Begin by selecting plants that are suitable for your climate and the amount of sunlight your space receives. Whether you choose to grow vegetables, herbs, or flowers, select plants that will thrive in your environment. Once you have your plants, invest in quality soil, containers, and gardening tools to ensure their success.

As your urban garden begins to flourish, take the time to nurture and care for your plants, enjoying the satisfaction that comes from watching them grow. Share your gardening journey with friends, family, or neighbors, and you may even inspire them to cultivate their green thumbs as well.

In conclusion, urban gardening is like painting a vibrant masterpiece on the canvas of a concrete jungle. It's a reminder that nature's beauty can thrive even in the busiest of cities, and your golden years are the perfect time to embrace this rewarding hobby. After all, these are your best years ahead, and with every seed you plant, you're sowing the foundation for a more beautiful and fulfilling life.

Category 3: Travel and Exploration

Bucket List # 17

Voluntourism: Travel with a Purpose

"The Best Way to find Yourself is to Lose Yourself in the Service of others."

– Mahatma Gandhi –

Voluntourism: Travel with a Purpose

Imagine exploring new places, meeting people from different cultures, and making a positive impact on the world, all while enjoying your golden years. Voluntourism, a combination of volunteering and tourism, offers the perfect opportunity to travel with a purpose, creating meaningful experiences that will enrich your life and the lives of those you help.

Voluntourism is important because it allows you to give back to communities in need, promote cross-cultural understanding, and develop new skills. Whether you're helping to build schools, teaching English, or supporting wildlife conservation efforts, your contributions can make a significant difference in the lives of those you serve.

To get started with voluntourism, begin by researching reputable organizations that offer volunteer opportunities in your areas of interest. Consider your skills, passions, and the level of physical activity required to ensure that you find a suitable project. Once you've found a program that aligns with your goals, connect with the organization and begin planning your trip.

During your voluntourism adventure, immerse yourself in the local culture, forge lasting connections with fellow volunteers, and embrace the challenges and rewards of making a difference. Remember to be open-minded and respectful, as your journey is not only about helping others but also learning and growing as an individual.

In conclusion, voluntourism is like weaving a colorful tapestry of experiences, where every thread represents a life touched, a lesson learned, and a memory cherished. Embrace this unique form of travel in your golden years and let it fill your heart with the joy of giving and the thrill of discovery. After all, these are your best years ahead, and with every new adventure, you're creating a legacy of compassion, understanding, and positive change.

Bucket List # 18

House Swapping: Embrace a Home Away from Home

"Adventure is a Path. Real Adventure, Self-determined, Self-motivated, often Risky, Forces you to have Firsthand Encounters with the World." – Mark Jenkins –

House Swapping: Embrace a Home Away from Home

Traveling and exploring new places is an exciting way to spend your golden years, but finding comfortable accommodations can sometimes be a challenge. House swapping is an innovative solution that allows you to enjoy the comforts of a home away from home while immersing yourself in the local culture.

House swapping is important because it provides a cost-effective and authentic travel experience. By exchanging homes with fellow travelers, you can save on accommodation expenses and enjoy the unique opportunity to live like a local. This allows you to truly appreciate the culture, customs, and everyday life of the places you visit.

To get started with house swapping, begin by researching reputable home exchange websites and platforms. Create a detailed profile, showcasing your home and its amenities, as well as the attractions and conveniences of your local area. Be honest about your preferences and expectations, and take the time to communicate with potential exchange partners to ensure a successful swap.

Before embarking on your house swapping adventure, prepare your home for your guests by cleaning, tidying, and securing any valuables. It's also a good idea to leave a guidebook or list of recommendations for your guests to help them make the most of their stay in your home. The process is simple: join a reputable house swapping platform, create an enticing profile showcasing your home, and start browsing for a perfect match.

In conclusion, house swapping is like exchanging keys to hidden treasure chests, each revealing a world of wonder and excitement waiting to be discovered. Embrace this unique travel experience in your golden years and let it unlock the door to authentic adventures and unforgettable memories. After all, these are your best years ahead, and with every home swap, you're stepping into a new and vibrant world, full of life and endless possibilities.

Bucket List # 19

Mystery Vacation: Let Fate Decide Your Destination

"Life is Either a Daring Adventure or Nothing at All." – Helen Keller –

In today's fast-paced world, we often forget the transformative power of a good book. If you're looking to inject some excitement and spontaneity into your golden years, it's time to consider a mystery vacation. Let fate decide your destination and embrace the thrilling unknown, discovering new places and experiences you may never have chosen for yourself.

A mystery vacation is a fantastic way to push yourself out of your comfort zone and embrace life's unpredictable nature. To get started, you can either book a package through a mystery travel agency or create your own surprise adventure. These agencies will handle all the planning for you, leaving you in suspense until the very last moment. Alternatively, you can ask a trusted friend or family member to plan your trip, keeping the destination a secret until it's time to depart.

The beauty of a mystery vacation lies in its uncertainty. You might find yourself exploring hidden gems in a small town or wandering the streets of a bustling city you've never heard of before. The important part is to let go of control, trust the process, and allow life's surprises to unfold before you.

In conclusion, imagine your life as a beautifully wrapped gift. A mystery vacation is like slowly peeling back the layers of wrapping paper, revealing the exciting and unexpected present that awaits inside. Embrace the adventure, cherish the memories, and let your golden years be filled with the joy of discovery. Remember, these are the best years of your life, so make every moment count by embarking on a thrilling mystery vacation. Dive into the pages of a good book and let the stories carry you away on a whirlwind of adventure, reminding you that life's greatest journeys are often found within the covers of a book.

Bucket List # 20

Cooking Classes Abroad: Master International Cuisine

"You don't have to Cook Fancy or Complicated Masterpieces – just Good food from Fresh Ingredients." – Julia Child –

As you embark on the journey of your golden years, why not explore the world of international cuisine by enrolling in cooking classes abroad? Learning to create delightful dishes from around the globe is not only a fun way to fill your days but also offers the chance to broaden your culinary horizons, make new friends, and immerse yourself in diverse cultures.

Taking cooking classes abroad allows you to delve deep into the heart of a country's customs and traditions, as you discover the rich history and unique flavors that define its cuisine. Whether you've always wanted to create authentic Spanish paella or master the art of French pastry, there's a world of mouthwatering experiences waiting for you.

To begin your gastronomic adventure, research reputable cooking schools or workshops in your dream destinations. Many of these establishments offer hands-on experiences, where you'll learn to prepare traditional dishes under the guidance of skilled chefs. As you sharpen your culinary talents, you'll also connect with fellow food enthusiasts, building friendships and memories that will last a lifetime.

Don't be afraid to step out of your comfort zone and experiment with new ingredients and techniques. Embrace the challenges and triumphs that come with mastering international cuisine, knowing that each dish you create is a reflection of your passion, curiosity, and zest for life.

In conclusion, think of your culinary journey as a colorful mosaic, with each international dish representing a unique piece that comes together to create a stunning masterpiece. As you explore the world through cooking classes, you'll enrich your life with a kaleidoscope of flavors and experiences that will add joy and excitement to your golden years. So, dear friends, let your taste buds lead the way on this delectable adventure, for these are the best years ahead of you.

Bucket List # 21

Literary Tours: Walk in the Footsteps of Famous Writers

"A Book is a Dream that you Hold in your Hand." – Neil Gaiman –

As you explore on the adventure of your golden years, consider exploring the enchanting world of literary tours. These unique journeys allow you to walk in the footsteps of famous writers, unveiling the places that inspired their masterpieces and offering a deeper connection with their work.

Literary tours are an exciting way to combine your love for literature with a passion for travel. You'll experience the magic of the settings that shaped your favorite stories, uncovering fascinating details about the authors' lives and the creative process behind their celebrated works.

To begin your literary pilgrimage, select a beloved author or a book that holds a special place in your heart. Research the locations that played a significant role in their life and work, and create an itinerary that highlights these literary landmarks. Many cities and towns offer guided tours dedicated to renowned writers, or you can curate your own bespoke journey using maps, guidebooks, and local advice.

Whether you're meandering through the Parisian streets that inspired Victor Hugo's "Les Misérables" or wandering the quaint English villages that served as a backdrop for Jane Austen's novels, literary tours provide a unique and captivating travel experience. You'll forge lasting memories and gain an even deeper appreciation for the authors and stories you cherish.

In conclusion, embarking on a literary tour is like stepping inside a beloved book and becoming a part of its enchanting world. As you traverse the landscapes that inspired your favorite writers, you'll weave a vivid tapestry of experiences that brings their stories to life in a whole new way. So, dear friends, seize this opportunity to celebrate the magic of literature during your golden years, for these are the best years ahead of you. Let the power of the written word transport you on a remarkable journey.

Bucket List # 22

Music Festival Hopping: Rock Out in Style

"Music Can Change the World because it can Change People." – Bono –

Explore on the exciting journey of your golden years, consider embracing the vibrant world of music festival hopping. These energetic events offer a unique opportunity to indulge your love for music, meet like-minded individuals, and experience the sheer joy of live performances in a whole new light.

Music festival hopping allows you to explore a wide variety of genres, discover emerging artists, and even travel to new and exciting destinations. With an array of festivals taking place around the globe, you have the chance to immerse yourself in diverse cultures and create memories that will last a lifetime.

To start your musical adventure, research music festivals that cater to your interests or spark your curiosity. From the iconic Glastonbury in England to the eclectic Coachella in California, there's a festival for every music enthusiast. Once you've chosen a few events that pique your interest, plan your trips around their dates and locations.

As you revel in the exhilaration of live music, you'll forge strong connections with fellow festivalgoers and create cherished memories that will resonate with you for years to come. Embrace the opportunity to let loose, dance, and celebrate the magic of music with newfound friends.

In conclusion, music festival hopping is like embarking on a thrilling treasure hunt through the realm of music, with each discovery revealing a new sound or rhythm that sets your soul alight. So, dear friends, dive headfirst into this electrifying adventure, for these are the best years ahead of you. Let the power of music guide you on a journey filled with laughter, joy, and unforgettable melodies, as you rock out in style and celebrate the soundtrack of your life.

Bucket List # 23

City Scavenger Hunts: Discover Hidden Gems

"Life is either a Daring Adventure or Nothing at all." – Helen Keller –

Explore on the thrilling journey of your golden years, consider exploring the hidden gems of cities around the world through engaging scavenger hunts. These lively adventures offer a unique way to dive into the rich history and culture of each destination, uncovering hidden treasures and creating unforgettable memories.

City scavenger hunts are an exciting opportunity to challenge yourself and learn something new while exploring unfamiliar places. You'll develop a deeper appreciation for each city's unique charm and character, as you navigate your way through winding streets and alleyways to discover lesser-known landmarks and attractions.

To begin your urban adventure, select a city that piques your curiosity or holds a special place in your heart. Research scavenger hunt companies that operate in your chosen destination, or create your own custom hunt using guidebooks, maps, and local recommendations. Be sure to include a mix of historical sites, cultural attractions, and local hotspots to create a well-rounded experience.

As you follow the clues and uncover hidden gems, you'll forge lasting memories and gain a newfound appreciation for the cities you explore. City scavenger hunts are not only a fun and interactive way to travel but also an opportunity to connect with fellow adventurers and share in the excitement of discovery.

In conclusion, embarking on a city scavenger hunt is like solving a captivating puzzle that reveals the true essence of each destination. As you piece together the clues and uncover each city's hidden treasures, you'll create a vivid tapestry of experiences that brings your travels to life in a whole new way. So, dear friends, seize this opportunity to transform your golden years into a grand adventure, for these are the best years ahead of you. Let your curiosity guide you as you unlock the mysteries of the world's most captivating cities, one scavenger hunt at a time.

Bucket List # 24

Themed Cruises: Sail Away on a Unique Voyage

"The World is a Book, and those Who do not Travel Read only One Page."

- Saint Augustine –

Experience on the exciting journey of your golden years, consider setting sail on a unique voyage by exploring the world of themed cruises. These captivating journeys offer a chance to combine your love for travel with your passions and interests, creating an unforgettable experience filled with fun, adventure, and like-minded companions.

Themed cruises cater to a wide range of interests, from culinary delights to musical extravaganzas, and everything in between. Whether you're a wine enthusiast, history buff, or dancing aficionado, there's a themed cruise out there that's tailor-made for you.

To begin your nautical adventure, research the various themed cruises available and select one that aligns with your interests or sparks your curiosity. Once you've found the perfect voyage, book your trip and start preparing for the journey of a lifetime. Be sure to pack appropriate attire, gear, and any other essentials that will enhance your experience onboard.

As you set sail on your themed cruise, you'll have the opportunity to immerse yourself in your chosen passion, attend workshops and seminars, and participate in themed activities and events. Along the way, you'll forge meaningful connections with fellow cruisers who share your interests, creating lasting memories and friendships that will enrich your golden years.

In conclusion, embarking on a themed cruise is like diving into a novel where each chapter reveals a new adventure tailored to your passions and interests. As you sail through the pages of this captivating story, you'll create a vivid tapestry of experiences that brings your golden years to life in a whole new way. So, dear friends, seize this opportunity to transform your retirement into a grand adventure, for these are the best years ahead of you. Let your passions guide you as you sail away on a unique voyage, exploring the world and yourself with every nautical mile.

Category 4: Learning and Growing

Bucket List # 25

Master a New Language: Unlock a World of Possibilities

"Learning Another Language is Like becoming Another Person." – Haruki Murakami –

Explore on the exciting journey of your golden years, consider unlocking a world of possibilities by mastering a new language. Learning a new language not only broadens your horizons but also stimulates your mind, fosters connections with people from diverse cultures, and adds an extra layer of excitement to your travels.

Taking on the challenge of learning a new language can be an enriching and rewarding experience. By immersing yourself in the intricacies of a foreign language, you'll develop a deeper understanding of the world around you and the people who inhabit it.

To get started, select a language that sparks your curiosity or holds a special place in your heart. Consider factors such as your travel plans, cultural interests, and personal goals when making your decision. Once you've chosen a language, explore various learning methods to find the one that suits you best. Options include enrolling in a local class, using language-learning apps, or participating in conversation exchanges with native speakers.

As you progress in your language-learning journey, embrace the opportunity to practice your newfound skills in real-life situations. Seek out local events, cultural centers, and language meetups where you can engage with native speakers and further hone your abilities.

In conclusion, mastering a new language is like acquiring a magical key that unlocks the doors to a world of new experiences and connections. As you journey through your golden years, this key will grant you access to an ever-expanding universe of possibilities, enriching your life in ways you never imagined. So, dear friends, seize this opportunity to transform your retirement into a grand adventure, for these are the best years ahead of you. Let the power of language guide you as you explore new lands, forge meaningful connections, and discover the endless potential that lies within you.

Bucket List # 26

Take Up an Instrument: Discover Your Musical Talent

"Music gives a Soul to the Universe, Wings to the Mind, Flight to the Imagination, and Life to Everything." – Plato –

Experience on the exciting journey of your golden years, consider tapping into the transformative power of music by learning to play an instrument. Discovering your musical talent not only brings joy and creativity into your life but also offers numerous benefits for your overall well-being, including improved cognitive function, enhanced coordination, and reduced stress.

Taking up an instrument can be a fulfilling and life-enriching experience. By dedicating time and effort to learning the art of music, you'll develop a new form of self-expression, allowing you to share your emotions, experiences, and stories in a unique and captivating way.

To get started, choose an instrument that speaks to your heart and resonates with your personal taste. Whether you're drawn to the melodic sound of the piano, the rich tones of the guitar, or the rhythmic beat of the drums, there's an instrument out there that's perfect for you. Once you've selected your instrument, explore various learning methods to find the one that suits your needs and preferences. Options include taking private lessons, attending group classes, or using online tutorials and instructional videos.

As you progress in your musical journey, embrace the opportunity to share your newfound talents with others. Seek out local open mic nights, community bands, or music clubs where you can perform, collaborate, and engage with fellow music enthusiasts.

In conclusion, learning to play an instrument is like being handed a paintbrush that allows you to create beautiful, colorful masterpieces on the canvas of your golden years. As you explore the vast landscape of music, you'll uncover hidden talents, forge meaningful connections, and infuse your retirement with a newfound sense of wonder and creativity. So, dear friends, seize this opportunity to transform your retirement into a grand symphony, for these are the best years ahead of you.

Bucket List # 27

Join a Book Club: Share Your Love for Literature

"A Book is a Dream that you Hold in your Hands." – Neil Gaiman –

Explore on the journey of your golden years, consider nurturing your love for literature by joining a book club. Book clubs provide a unique opportunity to share your passion for reading, engage in thought-provoking discussions, and form lasting friendships with fellow book lovers.

Joining a book club has numerous benefits. Not only will you be introduced to new and diverse books, but you'll also have the chance to delve deeper into the stories by engaging in lively discussions. These conversations can help sharpen your critical thinking skills, broaden your horizons, and provide a richer understanding of the world around you.

To begin your book club adventure, explore local libraries, community centers, or online platforms to find a group that aligns with your interests. Whether you're passionate about mystery novels, historical fiction, or non-fiction, there's a book club out there tailored to your literary tastes. Embrace the opportunity to participate actively in discussions, share your insights, and be open to differing perspectives.

If you're feeling particularly ambitious, consider starting your own book club. This allows you to handpick the members and shape the group according to your vision. You can invite friends, family, or fellow retirees who share your enthusiasm for literature, and together, you can embark on a literary journey filled with captivating stories, engaging discussions, and unforgettable memories.

Joining a book club is like venturing on a literary expedition with a group of fellow explorers. Each book you read together becomes a new destination to discover, filled with fascinating characters, compelling stories, and rich cultural landscapes. As you navigate this incredible journey, you'll forge meaningful connections with your fellow book lovers, enriching your golden years with the warmth of friendship and the joy of shared experiences. Open the book of your retirement and write a captivating chapter filled with the enchanting world of literature, for these are the best years ahead of you.

Bucket List # 28

Attend TED Talks: Get Inspired by Brilliant Minds

"The Only way to do Great Work is to Love What you do."
– Steve Jobs –

Retirement is a time for personal growth and rediscovery, and attending TED Talks can be an inspiring way to learn new ideas and expand your knowledge. TED Talks are short, powerful presentations given by some of the world's most brilliant minds, covering a wide range of topics, from science and technology to art and culture. By attending these talks, you can ignite your curiosity, stimulate your intellect, and get inspired to pursue your passions.

Attending TED Talks is a fantastic way to keep your mind sharp and engaged during your golden years. Each talk is designed to challenge your thinking, introduce new perspectives, and encourage you to explore fresh ideas. As you listen to these captivating speakers, you may find yourself inspired to take up new hobbies, engage in lifelong learning, or pursue a cause that is close to your heart.

To get started, search for TED events happening near you or watch TED Talks online. Many local universities, community centers, and organizations host TEDx events, which are independently organized

TED-like conferences. Attend these events to connect with like-minded individuals, engage in thought-provoking conversations, and discover new interests.

If you're unable to attend live events, you can still benefit from the wealth of knowledge shared in TED Talks by watching videos online. TED.com features thousands of recorded talks that can be accessed for free, allowing you to explore your interests and learn at your own pace.

Attending TED Talks is like planting seeds of knowledge in the garden of your mind. As you nurture these seeds with curiosity and passion, they will grow into a beautiful, flourishing landscape filled with new ideas, perspectives, and inspiration. Embrace this opportunity to cultivate your intellect and enrich your golden years, for these are the best years ahead of you.

Bucket List # 29

Learn to Dance: Move to the Rhythm of Life

"Life is the Dancer, and You are the Dance." – Eckhart Tolle –

Shake off the cobwebs of routine and step into the exciting world of dance! As you embark on this new chapter of your life, you deserve to feel the thrill of movement and the joy of self-expression. Learning to dance is not only a delightful way to reconnect with your body and soul, but it also offers numerous health and social benefits that will enrich your golden years.

Dancing is a fantastic way to stay active and healthy as it improves flexibility, balance, and muscle strength. Additionally, it offers a natural remedy to reduce stress and boost mood, as moving to music releases those feel-good endorphins. As you sway to the rhythm of life, you'll also forge new connections with like-minded people, creating a sense of community and belonging.

Getting started is easier than you think! Start by exploring different dance styles to find the one that resonates with you. From ballroom and salsa to line dancing and Zumba, the choices are limitless. Next, look for local dance classes or workshops, which are often available at community centers, gyms, or dance studios. If you prefer learning at your own pace, consider online tutorials or instructional DVDs.

Remember, it's never too late to learn and enjoy dancing. Begin with an open mind, and don't be afraid to make mistakes. The key is to have fun and let your inner dancer shine. As you progress, you'll find yourself becoming more confident, agile, and expressive, both on and off the dance floor.

Dancing is like a colorful bouquet of flowers - each step and twirl adds a vibrant petal to your life, creating a beautiful arrangement that reflects your unique journey. Let loose, embrace the rhythm, and dance your way into the best years of your life.

Bucket List # 30

Creative Writing Workshops: Pen Your Own Masterpiece

"The Pen is Mightier than the Sword." – Edward Bulwer-Lytton –

Unleash the power of your imagination and embark on a literary adventure through creative writing workshops! Whether you have a story that's been brewing inside you for years or simply want to explore a new form of self-expression, there's no better time than now to pen your own masterpiece. In your golden years, you have a treasure trove of experiences, wisdom, and memories to share with the world.

Creative writing offers a multitude of benefits, such as honing communication skills, boosting self-esteem, and providing a therapeutic outlet for emotions. It allows you to create your own world, giving you the freedom to invent characters, explore new ideas, and craft powerful narratives. Plus, it's an excellent way to keep your brain sharp and engaged.

To begin your literary journey, research local creative writing workshops, which can often be found at community centers, libraries, or bookstores. If you prefer a more flexible schedule, online courses or writing groups can offer support and guidance from the comfort of your own home. Regardless of the format, connecting with like-minded individuals will inspire and motivate you as you hone your craft.

As you embark on this new adventure, remember that the beauty of creative writing lies in the process, not just the final product. Embrace your unique voice and style, and don't be afraid to experiment. With dedication and persistence, you'll soon find your words flowing effortlessly onto the page.

Think of your creative writing journey as a colorful quilt, with each word and sentence a vibrant patch that comes together to form a stunning work of art. As you stitch together your life experiences, emotions, and imagination, you're not only creating a masterpiece but also weaving the fabric of your golden years.

Bucket List # 31

DIY Home Improvement: Tackle Your Dream Projects

"Your Home should tell the Story of who you are, and be a Collection of what you Love."

–Nate Berkus –

Transform your living space into a true reflection of your personality and passions with DIY home improvement projects! Retirement presents the perfect opportunity to tackle those dream projects you've always wanted to pursue, allowing you to create an environment that both inspires and comforts you.

Engaging in DIY home improvement not only helps you personalize your home, but also promotes mental and physical well-being. As you plan, create, and problem-solve, you'll keep your mind sharp and active, while the physical labor involved contributes to a healthy and active lifestyle. Moreover, the satisfaction of completing a project with your own hands is immensely rewarding and boosts self-confidence.

To get started, make a list of projects you'd like to tackle, from small fixes and updates to more significant renovations. Prioritize them based on factors such as budget, time, and personal preference. Next, research each project to determine the necessary tools, materials, and skills required. Many online resources, books, and magazines offer step-by-step guides and helpful tips for various home improvement endeavors.

As you explore on your DIY journey, remember to be patient and take the time to learn new skills. Don't be afraid to ask for help or advice from friends, family, or even professionals. The key is to enjoy the process and take pride in the fruits of your labor.

Think of your DIY home improvement projects as a beautiful mosaic, with each tile representing a unique piece of your personality, interests, and experiences. As you skillfully arrange and assemble these pieces, you create a masterpiece that not only reflects who you are but also serves as a testament to your dedication and creativity. Embrace this opportunity to make your golden years truly shine.

Bucket List # 32

Pottery Classes: Shape and Create Your Own Masterpieces

"The Aim of Art is to Represent not the outward Appearance of Things, but their inward Significance." – Aristotle –

Unearth your inner artist and explore the captivating world of pottery! Engaging in pottery classes offers a unique opportunity to shape and create your own masterpieces while fostering self-expression and relaxation. As you embrace your golden years, let your hands and imagination mold stunning works of art, inspired by your wealth of experiences and creativity.

Pottery is not only a delightful way to spend your time, but it also provides numerous mental and physical benefits. Working with clay allows you to unleash your creative potential while improving focus and concentration. Moreover, the tactile nature of pottery can be therapeutic, helping to relieve stress and anxiety. As you hone your skills, you'll also strengthen your hand-eye coordination and dexterity.

To begin your artistic journey, research local pottery classes or workshops at art centers, community colleges, or pottery studios. Many of these venues offer beginner-friendly courses that will introduce you to various techniques, materials, and tools. Alternatively, you may consider online tutorials or instructional videos if you prefer learning at your own pace.

As you delve into the world of pottery, remember to be patient with yourself and to embrace the learning process. Cherish the freedom to experiment, and don't be afraid to make mistakes. With practice and perseverance, you'll soon find your hands skillfully shaping clay into stunning creations.

Pottery is like a garden, with each piece you create akin to a beautiful, blossoming flower. As you nurture your skills and allow your creativity to bloom, you cultivate a vibrant artistic landscape that reflects the passion and vitality of your golden years. Your pottery journey as a river, meandering through the landscape of your golden years. You'll discover new techniques, styles, and inspirations that enrich your creative flow. As the river widens and deepens, so too does your artistic prowess, culminating in a breathtaking body of work that reflects the essence of your unique journey.

Category 5: Connecting with Others

Bucket List # 33

Host a Themed Dinner Party: A Night of Fun and Flavors

"One Cannot think well, Love well, Sleep well, if one has not Dined well."

– Virginia Woolf –

Explore your golden years with an exciting twist on traditional gatherings by hosting a themed dinner party. A night filled with laughter, conversation, and delectable flavors, themed dinner parties offer an incredible opportunity to create cherished memories and strengthen bonds with friends and family.

Hosting a themed dinner party not only adds an element of fun to your social life but also allows you to showcase your creativity in the kitchen. As you explore various culinary styles, you'll broaden your cooking skills and knowledge, delighting your taste buds and those of your guests. Moreover, themed dinner parties' foster connection, allowing guests to share stories, experiences, and laughter, enriching your life and the lives of your loved ones.

To plan your unforgettable themed dinner party, start by choosing a theme that speaks to your interests and passions. Whether it's a

Hawaiian luau, a 1920s speakeasy, or a night of Mediterranean flavors, the possibilities are boundless. Once you've decided on a theme, create a menu that features dishes and drinks that capture the essence of your chosen concept. Don't forget to consider decorations and attire to fully immerse your guests in the experience.

As you prepare for your themed dinner party, remember to have fun and let your creativity shine. Don't be afraid to think outside the box or ask for help from friends and family. The key is to create a memorable and enjoyable experience for everyone involved.

Hosting a themed dinner party is like painting a vibrant scene on a canvas, with each dish and decorative element a stroke of color that brings the masterpiece to life. As you curate these delightful experiences, you're not only filling your golden years with joy and laughter, but you're also creating a beautiful collection of memories that will be cherished for years to come.

Bucket List # 34

Start a Social Club: Connect with Like-Minded Individuals

"Alone, we can do so Little; Together, we can do so much."
– Helen Keller –

In your golden years, there's no better time to celebrate friendship, camaraderie, and shared passions by starting a social club. Connecting with like-minded individuals through common interests and activities not only enriches your life but also fosters meaningful relationships that stand the test of time.

Starting a social club offers numerous benefits, such as combating loneliness, expanding your social circle, and providing a sense of belonging. By pursuing shared hobbies and interests, you'll strengthen bonds with others, creating a support network that uplifts and inspires. Moreover, social clubs offer the opportunity to learn new skills, discover hidden talents, and engage in stimulating conversations that keep your mind sharp and active.

To begin your social club adventure, identify a theme or activity that resonates with your interests and passions. Whether it's a book club, gardening group, photography club, or knitting circle, the possibilities are endless. Next, reach out to friends, neighbors, and community members who share your enthusiasm, and invite them to join your club. You can also promote your club through local bulletin boards, community centers, or social media platforms.

As you experience on this journey, remember that the key to a successful social club is creating a welcoming and inclusive environment. Be open to new ideas and perspectives, and encourage everyone to contribute their unique talents and experiences. By fostering a sense of community and connection, your social club will flourish and thrive.

Starting a social club is like planting a lush, vibrant garden, with each member a unique and beautiful flower. As you nurture your club with friendship, shared experiences, and laughter, the garden blossoms, creating a sanctuary of color, joy, and camaraderie. Embrace this opportunity to cultivate the garden of your golden years and watch as it blossoms into a breathtaking masterpiece that celebrates the best years of your life.

Bucket List # 35

Participate in a Charity Event: Make a Difference Together

"No Act of Kindness, No Matter how Small, is Ever Wasted." – Aesop –

Your golden years present the perfect opportunity to make a meaningful impact on the world around you by participating in charity events. Whether it's a walkathon, food drive, or volunteering at a local shelter, these events provide a chance to join forces with others, create lasting memories, and contribute to a greater cause.

Participating in charity events not only benefits those in need but also enriches your own life. By dedicating your time and energy to help others, you'll experience a sense of fulfillment, purpose, and joy. Furthermore, charity events offer the opportunity to connect with like-minded individuals, forging bonds of friendship and solidarity through your shared commitment to making a difference.

To get started, research local charity events or organizations that align with your values and interests. Many non-profits and community organizations host events throughout the year, catering to various causes and initiatives. Once you've found an event that resonates with you, reach out to the organizers to learn how you can get involved. You can also invite friends and family to join you, creating an even more significant impact and shared experience.

As you embark on this journey of giving, remember that every act of kindness, no matter how small, contributes to the greater good. Embrace the spirit of generosity and let it fill your heart with warmth and compassion.

Participating in charity events is like weaving a vibrant tapestry of kindness and compassion. Each thread represents an act of giving, and as these threads intertwine, they create a beautiful pattern that reflects the love and care you've shared with others. By weaving this tapestry throughout your golden years, you'll not only create a lasting legacy of goodwill but also celebrate the best years of your life, filled with warmth, connection, and purpose.

Bucket List # 36

Take Up Improv: Embrace Spontaneity and Laughter

"Life is 10% what Happens to you and 90% how you React to it." – Charles R. Swindoll –

In your golden years, embrace spontaneity, laughter, and the joy of living in the moment by taking up improv. Improvisational theater, or improv for short, is a form of theater where most or all of the performance is created spontaneously, without a script. By participating in improv, you'll have the opportunity to sharpen your wit, think on your feet, and cultivate a sense of humor that will enrich your life and the lives of those around you.

Taking up improv offers numerous benefits, such as enhancing your communication skills, boosting self-confidence, and encouraging creative thinking. As you engage in improvised scenes and games, you'll learn to adapt to unexpected situations, find humor in the ordinary, and develop a deeper connection with your fellow performers. Furthermore, improv is an excellent way to stay socially active and connected, as it fosters a supportive and collaborative environment where everyone can thrive.

To get started, look for local improv classes, workshops, or groups in your community. Many theaters and community centers offer classes catered to individuals of all experience levels. Don't be afraid to step out of your comfort zone and give it a try – remember, the spirit of improv is all about embracing the unexpected and having fun.

As you explore on your improv journey, keep an open mind and a playful attitude. Embrace the opportunity to grow, learn, and laugh with others, as you create unforgettable memories and fill your golden years with joy and laughter.

Taking up improv is like embarking on a thrilling roller coaster ride. As the ride twists and turns, you'll encounter surprising moments that leave you breathless with laughter and exhilaration. By embracing the spontaneity of improv, you'll infuse your golden years with excitement and adventure, creating a vibrant and fulfilling chapter of your life that celebrates the best years yet to come.

Bucket List # 37

Join a Local Sports League: Foster Team Spirit

"Unity is Strength... When there is Teamwork and Collaboration, Wonderful things can be Achieved." – Mattie Stepanek –

As you explore on your golden years, consider joining a local sports league to foster team spirit, stay active, and make lasting memories with friends old and new. Participating in team sports offers numerous benefits, such as improving physical health, enhancing social connections, and promoting a sense of camaraderie and accomplishment.

Joining a local sports league allows you to engage in friendly competition while also building valuable teamwork skills. Whether it's a casual game of softball, bowling, or even pickleball, the thrill of working together towards a common goal creates a bond that lasts a lifetime. Moreover, team sports provide the opportunity to challenge yourself, set goals, and celebrate personal milestones and achievements.

To get started, research local sports leagues and clubs in your community that cater to your interests and abilities. Many organizations offer recreational leagues tailored to individuals of all experience levels and age groups. Once you've found a league that aligns with your interests, reach out to the organizers to learn how you can get involved. Don't hesitate to invite friends and family to join you on this journey, creating an even more enjoyable and supportive experience.

As you embrace the spirit of teamwork and friendly competition, remember that the key to success in team sports is collaboration, communication, and mutual support. By fostering an environment of encouragement and camaraderie, you'll create a vibrant and fulfilling chapter of your life that celebrates the best years ahead.

Joining a local sports league is like assembling a vibrant mosaic, with each teammate representing a unique and colorful piece. As you work together and support one another, the pieces come together to form a beautiful masterpiece that represents the power of unity and collaboration. Embrace this opportunity to create lasting memories and connections that enrich your golden years, reminding you that the best is yet to come.

Bucket List # 38

Attend a Cultural Festival: Immerse Yourself in Diversity

"Life is a Great big Canvas, and you should throw all the Paint on it you can."

– Danny Kaye –

Imagine yourself immersed in a sea of colors, sounds, and flavors, as you dance to the rhythm of a new culture. Attending a cultural festival is an exhilarating way to breathe life into your golden years and celebrate the diversity that our world has to offer.

Why is it important to attend a cultural festival? As you enter this exciting phase of your life, broadening your horizons and embracing new experiences can bring renewed purpose and joy. Cultural festivals are a fantastic opportunity to learn about different traditions, meet interesting people, and create lasting memories. By participating in these events, you are not only enriching your own life but also fostering understanding and respect among different cultures.

How can you get started? First, do some research to discover the cultural festivals that resonate with you the most. Festivals can range from local events celebrating your own community's heritage to international extravaganzas showcasing art, music, and dance from around the world. Once you have a few options in mind, plan your visit well in advance, taking into consideration factors such as location, accommodations, and accessibility. Remember to pack an open mind, a sense of adventure, and a willingness to try new things.

In the end, attending a cultural festival is like adding a vibrant splash of color to the canvas of your life. Each new experience is a brushstroke, painting a masterpiece of memories that you can look back on with a smile. Your golden years are a blank canvas, and it's up to you to make them as vivid and exciting as possible.

Go ahead and throw all the paint you can on the canvas of life by attending a cultural festival. Let the colors of the world blend together and create a beautiful, harmonious masterpiece that will remind you that these are, indeed, your best years ahead

Bucket List # 39

Organize a Game Night: Bond Over Friendly Competition

"Play is our Brain's Favorite way of Learning." – Diane Ackerman –

Picture this: A room filled with laughter and friendly banter, the clinking of glasses, and the sound of dice hitting the table. A game night is the perfect way to bond with friends and family while engaging in some healthy competition. During your golden years, organizing a game night can bring you closer to your loved ones, provide entertainment, and keep your mind sharp.

Why is organizing a game night important? As we age, staying socially active and maintaining strong connections with friends and family is crucial for our overall well-being. Game nights offer an opportunity to strengthen these bonds while having a blast. Plus, many games require strategic thinking and problem-solving skills, which can help keep your brain in tip-top shape.

How can you get started? First, choose a date and time that works best for everyone, and then send out invitations. Next, decide on a selection of games that cater to various interests and skill levels. Classic board games, card games, and trivia games are always popular choices. Don't forget to prepare some snacks and beverages to keep everyone fueled for a night of fun.

As you plan your game night, remember that the key to success is creating an inviting atmosphere where everyone feels welcome and encouraged to participate. Emphasize that the goal is to have fun and enjoy each other's company, rather than focusing solely on winning.

Organizing a game night is like baking a batch of cookies. The ingredients—games, friends, and family—come together to create something warm, sweet, and satisfying. When you share these cookies, or in this case, the experience of a game night, you're spreading joy, nourishing relationships, and making lasting memories. Plan that game night, roll the dice, and let the laughter and camaraderie remind you that these are truly the best years of your life.

Bucket List # 40

Try Speed-Friending: Expand Your Social Circle

"Each Friend Represents a World in us, a world Possibly not Born until they arrive, and it is only by this Meeting that a New World is Born." – Anaïs Nin –

Imagine walking into a room filled with smiling faces, laughter, and the buzz of energetic conversations. Speed-friending is an exciting and unconventional way to expand your social circle and create new connections during your golden years.

As we explore on our retirement journey, cultivating new friendships can bring fresh perspectives, spark joy, and provide support during this exciting phase of life. Speed-friending offers a fun and efficient way to meet like-minded individuals, allowing you to cast a wide net and discover potential friends with shared interests and hobbies.

How can you get started? First, search online or inquire at local community centers and senior clubs to find speed-friending events in your area. These events are typically well-organized, with structured conversation prompts and timed rounds to ensure everyone gets a chance to connect with each other. Before attending, prepare a few interesting questions or topics to help spark conversation and show genuine interest in getting to know others. Most importantly, bring your best smile and an open mind to make the most of this unique experience.

Trying speed-friending is like planting a garden of friendship. Each new connection is a seed, and with time, care, and nurturing, these seeds can grow into beautiful, flourishing relationships. As you tend to your friendship garden, you'll be rewarded with a vibrant, diverse network of people who can enrich your life and make your golden years truly unforgettable.

Take the leap and embrace the exciting world of speed-friending. Allow your heart to overflow with love and laughter as you meet new friends and create lasting memories together. Remember, your best years are still ahead, and they're waiting for you to fill them with joy, adventure, and the warmth of friendship.

Category 6: Health and Wellness Adventures

Bucket List # 41

Join a Laughter Club: Embrace the Power of Joy

"Laughter is the Sun that Drives Winter from the Human Face." – Victor Hugo –

Picture a group of people gathered together, their faces beaming with joy as laughter echoes through the air. A laughter club is a unique and uplifting way to embrace the power of joy during your golden years, bringing happiness and camaraderie to your everyday life.

Why is joining a laughter club important? Laughter has numerous health benefits, including reducing stress, boosting mood, and improving heart health. Moreover, it helps you connect with others, creating a sense of belonging and shared joy. In your golden years, a laughter club can become a source of positivity, well-being, and lasting friendships.

How can you get started? Begin by searching online or asking at local community centers for laughter clubs in your area. These clubs usually meet regularly and are led by a laughter leader who guides the group through a series of laughter exercises and breathing techniques. When attending your first laughter club meeting, come with an open mind and a willingness to embrace the contagious power of laughter.

As you participate in laughter club sessions, let go of any inhibitions and allow yourself to fully experience the joy of laughing with others. Remember, laughter is a universal language that can bridge gaps and bring people together, creating bonds that last a lifetime.

Joining a laughter club is like planting a tree that blossoms with joy. As the tree grows, its branches reach out, touching the lives of those around it and creating a canopy of happiness that shelters everyone. By nurturing this tree and cherishing the laughter it brings, you'll create a sanctuary of positivity and well-being during your golden years.

Continue your laughter club adventure and let the waves of joy carry you forward. Embrace the power of laughter and let it remind you that your best years are still ahead, filled with boundless happiness, love, and unforgettable memories.

Bucket List # 42

Try a New Fitness Class: Challenge Your Body and Mind

"Your Body can do it. It's your Mind you Need to Convince." – Anonymous –

Envision yourself stepping onto the floor of a new fitness class, your heart pounding with anticipation as the music begins to play. Trying a new fitness class is a fantastic way to challenge your body and mind, keeping you active and engaged during your golden years.

Why is trying a new fitness class important? Staying physically active is essential for maintaining overall health and well-being as we age. Trying a new fitness class not only helps you build strength and flexibility but also provides mental stimulation and social interaction. Additionally, exploring different types of exercise can keep your workout routine fresh and exciting, making it more enjoyable and easier to stick to.

Begin by researching local gyms, community centers, or senior clubs that offer fitness classes catering to a variety of interests and abilities. You might consider trying yoga, Pilates, dance classes, or even water aerobics. When selecting a class, consider your current fitness level, any health concerns, and your personal preferences.

Once you've chosen a class, make sure to bring comfortable clothing, a water bottle, and a positive attitude. Be patient with yourself as you learn new moves and techniques, and don't be afraid to ask for assistance or modifications if needed. Remember, the goal is to enjoy the experience and reap the benefits of staying active.

Trying a new fitness class is like embarking on an adventure through uncharted territory. Each step you take, each new move you learn, adds to the excitement and richness of your journey. As you conquer challenges and overcome obstacles, you'll emerge stronger, more confident, and ready to tackle whatever comes your way.

Step out of your comfort zone and try a new fitness class. Explore the challenge, and let it remind you that your best years are still ahead, filled with boundless energy, vitality, and the joy of discovering new ways to stay healthy and active.

Bucket List # 43

Attend a Wellness Retreat: Nourish Your Body, Mind, and Soul

"Take Care of your Body. It's the only Place you have to Live." – Jim Rohn –

Imagine yourself stepping into a tranquil oasis, surrounded by nature's beauty, where the focus is on nurturing and nourishing your body, mind, and soul. Attending a wellness retreat offers the perfect opportunity to recharge, rejuvenate, and invest in your well-being during your golden years.

Why is attending a wellness retreat important? As we age, it becomes increasingly crucial to prioritize our health and well-being. A wellness retreat offers a dedicated space and time for you to focus on self-care, relaxation, and personal growth. You'll have the chance to learn new practices, try different treatments, and explore various activities that promote a healthy, balanced lifestyle.

How can you get started? Begin by researching wellness retreats that cater to your specific interests and needs. There are countless options available, from yoga and meditation retreats to those focused on nutrition, fitness, or even holistic healing. Consider factors such as location, duration, and budget when making your decision.

Once you've selected a retreat, prepare yourself for the experience by setting intentions for what you hope to achieve during your time there. This might include goals related to physical health, mental clarity, or personal growth. Approach the retreat with an open mind and a willingness to embrace new experiences and perspectives.

Attending a wellness retreat is like stepping into a sanctuary where you can replenish your inner reserves and cultivate a deep sense of balance and harmony. As you immerse yourself in this transformative environment, you'll emerge revitalized and equipped with the tools and knowledge to maintain your well-being for years to come.

Keep attending wellness retreats and let them nourish your body, mind, and soul. Let these experiences serve as a reminder that your best years are still ahead, filled with balance, vitality, and the joy of living life in harmony with yourself and the world around you.

Bucket List # 44

Take a Meditation Course: Cultivate Inner Peace

"Peace Comes from within. Do not Seek it Without." – Buddha –

Picture yourself sitting in a serene space, eyes closed, as you take slow, deep breaths and let go of the thoughts and worries that fill your mind. Taking a meditation course offers the perfect opportunity to cultivate inner peace and discover the benefits of mindfulness during your golden years.

Why is taking a meditation course important? As we age, it becomes increasingly vital to find ways to manage stress and promote mental well-being. Meditation offers a powerful tool for enhancing focus, reducing anxiety, and fostering a sense of inner calm. By taking a meditation course, you'll learn techniques and practices that can help you navigate the challenges of life with grace and poise.

How can you get started? Begin by researching meditation courses available in your area or online. You might consider enrolling in a local class, attending a meditation retreat, or exploring online resources such as apps or video tutorials. When selecting a course, consider factors such as the teaching style, duration, and any specific meditation techniques you'd like to learn.

Once you've chosen a meditation course, commit to regular practice and approach the process with an open mind and a willingness to explore your inner world. Be patient with yourself as you learn new techniques and remember that progress in meditation takes time and dedication.

Taking a meditation course is like planting a seed of tranquility within your soul. As you nurture this seed through regular practice, it grows into a strong, deep-rooted tree of inner peace that provides shelter from the storms of life. Each time you meditate, you water the tree, ensuring it continues to thrive and flourish.

Take the plunge and enroll in a meditation course. Let the practice of mindfulness guide you towards inner peace and serve as a reminder that your best years are still ahead, filled with calmness, clarity, and the joy of living life in harmony with yourself and the world around you.

Bucket List # 45

Participate in a Silent Disco: Dance to Your Own Beat

"Dance is the Hidden Language of the Soul." – Martha Graham –

Picture yourself moving to the beat of your favorite tunes, surrounded by fellow dance enthusiasts, all wearing headphones and grooving to their own personal soundtrack. Participating in a silent disco offers a unique and exhilarating way to enjoy music, dance, and social connection during your golden years.

Why is participating in a silent disco important? Dancing has numerous physical and mental health benefits, such as improved balance, coordination, and mood. Silent discos take the experience to a new level by allowing you to customize your music, volume, and tempo, making it a truly personalized and inclusive activity.

How can you get started? Research silent disco events happening in your area or nearby cities. These events are often hosted at various venues, such as community centers, parks, or even art galleries. If you can't find any local events, consider organizing your own silent disco with friends, family, or community members. You'll need wireless headphones and a source of music, such as smartphones or portable music players with customizable playlists.

Once you've found or organized a silent disco, let loose and have fun. Embrace the opportunity to dance like nobody's watching and enjoy the company of others who share your enthusiasm for music and movement. Don't be afraid to experiment with different genres, tempos, and dance styles, as the beauty of a silent disco lies in its versatility and personalization.

Participating in a silent disco is like entering a world were music and movement flow together in perfect harmony. As you dance to your own beat, you'll discover new layers of self-expression, joy, and connection that infuse your golden years with a vibrant energy.

Put on those headphones and step onto the dance floor. Let the silent disco experience serve as a reminder that your best years are still ahead, filled with laughter, fun, and the joy of living life to the beat of your own unique rhythm.

Bucket List # 46

Explore Aromatherapy: Delight in the World of Scents

"Smell is a Potent Wizard that Transports you Across Thousands of Miles and all the Years you have Lived." – Helen Keller –

Imagine yourself enveloped by the soothing scent of lavender, or the invigorating aroma of citrus, as your senses come alive and your mood lifts. Exploring aromatherapy offers a delightful way to experience the world of scents and discover the therapeutic benefits of essential oils during your golden years.

Why is exploring aromatherapy important? Aromatherapy harnesses the power of natural plant extracts, using their aromatic properties to enhance emotional, mental, and physical well-being. By incorporating aromatherapy into your daily routine, you can create a personalized sensory experience that promotes relaxation, focus, or revitalization, depending on your needs and preferences.

How can you get started? Begin by researching essential oils and their various properties. Some popular oils include lavender for relaxation, peppermint for focus, and lemon for energy. Once you've identified a few scents that appeal to you, purchase high-quality essential oils from a reputable supplier.

Next, explore different ways to incorporate aromatherapy into your life. You might consider using a diffuser to disperse the scent throughout a room, adding a few drops to a warm bath, or creating a scented massage oil. As you experiment, take note of how each scent affects your mood and well-being.

As you delve into the world of aromatherapy, consider sharing your newfound knowledge and experiences with friends and family. Host a scented gathering or create personalized scent blends as gifts, fostering connections and shared enjoyment of this fascinating sensory journey.

Exploring aromatherapy is like uncovering a hidden garden of sensory delights, where each aroma carries its own unique story and evokes a distinct emotional response. As you wander through this garden, you'll discover new ways to enhance your well-being and bring joy to your golden years.

Immerse yourself in the world of scents and let aromatherapy guide you on a sensory adventure. Allow this exploration to serve as a reminder that your best years are still ahead, filled with wonder, discovery, and the joy of living life in harmony with your senses.

Bucket List # 47

Try Tai Chi or Qigong: Balance Your Energy Flow

"Tai Chi does not mean Oriental Wisdom or Something Exotic. It is the Wisdom of your Own senses, your own mind and Body Together as one Process." – Chungliang Al Huang –

Explore the gentle, flowing movements of Tai Chi or Qigong, ancient Chinese practices that offer a unique way to cultivate balance, relaxation, and overall wellness during your golden years. These mindful exercises focus on the harmonious flow of energy, or "Qi," within the body, helping you to achieve greater physical and emotional well-being.

Why are Tai Chi and Qigong important? These practices offer a low-impact, holistic approach to fitness, combining elements of meditation, breathing techniques, and movement. Regular practice can improve balance, flexibility, and mental clarity, while reducing stress and promoting a sense of inner peace.

How can you get started? Research local classes or workshops in your area, as learning from a qualified instructor is the best way to master the basic movements and principles. Alternatively, you can explore online resources, such as instructional videos or articles, to begin your journey at home. Tai Chi and Qigong can be practiced alone or with a group, so consider inviting friends or family to join you in this transformative experience.

As you delve deeper into Tai Chi and Qigong, you'll discover a wealth of variations and styles to explore, allowing you to tailor your practice to suit your personal needs and preferences. Embrace the opportunity to learn from different teachers and fellow practitioners, continually refining your understanding and technique.

Practicing Tai Chi or Qigong is like embarking on a voyage along a gently meandering river, where each bend reveals new insights and discoveries about yourself and the world around you. As you navigate this tranquil journey, you'll find greater balance, harmony, and vitality, enhancing the quality of your golden years.

Step onto the path of Tai Chi and Qigong and let these ancient practices guide you toward a more balanced, fulfilling life. Remember that your best years are still ahead, filled with growth, exploration, and the joy of living life in harmony with your body, mind, and spirit.

Bucket List # 48

Experience Sound Healing: Discover the Power of Vibrations

"Life is Like a Piano. What you Get out of it Depends on how you Play it." – Tom Lehrer –

Adventurous souls, to the world of sound healing. When we think about the ultimate retirement bucket list, experiencing sound healing should be at the top of your list. Imagine unlocking the power of vibrations to rejuvenate your mind, body, and soul. As you embark on this journey, you'll discover that it's not just about relaxation, but also about self-discovery and finding harmony within yourself.

Sound healing is an ancient practice that utilizes various frequencies and vibrations to create harmony within our body, mind, and spirit. These vibrations, produced by instruments like singing bowls, tuning forks, and gongs, can help alleviate stress, improve focus, and stimulate the body's natural healing processes

How can you get started with sound healing? Look for local sound healing workshops or classes in your community, or even online. Many wellness centers and yoga studios offer sessions specifically designed for seniors, providing a welcoming and supportive environment for you to explore this ancient practice. Alternatively, you can also purchase your own sound healing instruments and learn to play them at home, creating your very own healing sanctuary.

Remember, there's no right or wrong way to experience sound healing. The key is to approach it with an open mind and a sense of curiosity. As you become more familiar with the different instruments and techniques, you'll find the perfect combination that resonates with you and allows you to tap into the healing power of sound.

As you embark on this journey, you'll discover that sound healing can be as therapeutic as it is fun. You might even find that you've uncovered a new passion or hobby to share with your friends and family.

To wrap it up, think of sound healing like tuning a musical instrument. Just as a finely tuned piano produces beautiful melodies, our bodies, when in harmony, create a symphony of health and well-being. Embrace this powerful practice and remember, your best years are just beginning. So go ahead, tune into the power of vibrations, and allow your golden years to sing with joy and vitality.

Category 7: Embracing Your Creative Side

Bucket List # 49

Join a Community Theater: Unleash Your Inner Thespian

"Age is an Issue of Mind over Matter. If you don't mind, it doesn't matter." – Mark Twain –

Golden years are the perfect time to explore new passions and rediscover the joy of living. One such adventure is joining a community theater, where you can unleash your inner thespian and create memories to last a lifetime. Not only will you be learning a new skill, but you'll also make new friends and find a sense of belonging.

Community theaters are welcoming environments for people of all ages and backgrounds. They offer a variety of roles, from acting on stage to helping behind the scenes. Whatever your level of experience, there is a place for you in this vibrant world. It is never too late to embrace the spotlight and feel the magic of theater.

To get started, search online or visit your local library to find community theaters in your area. Attend a few performances to get a sense of their style and atmosphere. Many theaters offer workshops and classes for beginners, providing a fantastic opportunity to learn the basics of acting and stagecraft.

Next, keep an eye on audition notices and sign up when a production piques your interest. Remember, even if you don't land a leading role, there are plenty of supporting roles and backstage opportunities that are just as rewarding. Embrace the journey, and you'll find your confidence soaring as you explore this new and exciting chapter of your life.

As you take center stage in your golden years, think of yourself as a caterpillar emerging from its chrysalis as a magnificent butterfly. Just like the butterfly, you are beginning a new and beautiful journey, full of color and excitement. Your best years are ahead of you, waiting to be filled with laughter, friendship, and the joy of the spotlight. Embrace your golden years and let your inner thespian shine!

Bucket List # 50

Create a Vision Board: Visualize Your Dreams and Goals

"The only Thing that Stands Between you and your Dream is the will to try and the Belief that it is Actually Possible." – Joel Brown –

Your golden years are an opportunity to pursue your dreams and goals with passion and enthusiasm. One creative and inspiring way to do this is by creating a vision board—a visual representation of your aspirations and the life you want to lead.

Creating a vision board serves as a constant reminder of what you want to achieve and helps you stay focused on your goals. Seeing your dreams laid out before you can motivate you to take action, turning your retirement into an exciting adventure full of personal growth and fulfillment.

To begin, gather magazines, newspapers, or printouts of images that represent your goals and desires. You can also include quotes, affirmations, or personal mementos that hold special meaning. Next, find a large poster board, corkboard, or even a digital platform to arrange your chosen items.

As you create your vision board, think about the areas of your life you want to focus on, such as travel, hobbies, family, or personal growth. Arrange the images and words in a way that feels inspiring and visually appealing. Place your vision board in a prominent spot where you can see it every day, serving as a daily reminder of your dreams.

Share your vision board with friends or family, inviting them to create their own. By supporting each other, you can make your golden years even more rewarding as you work together to achieve your goals.

Imagine your retirement as a blank canvas, and your vision board as the palette of colors you will use to paint the masterpiece of your golden years. Each image, quote, and affirmation is a vibrant hue that will bring life and energy to your days. The more colors you add to your palette, the richer and more vivid your masterpiece will become.

Remember, your best years are ahead of you. With a vision board, you can transform your dreams into reality, creating a life full of joy, excitement, and personal fulfillment.

Bucket List # 51

Start a Photography Project: Capture the Beauty of Everyday Life

"Life is like a Camera. Focus on what's Important, Capture the Good Times, develop from the Negatives, and if things don't work out, take another shot." – Unknown –

Hello, my adventurous retirees! Are you ready to embark on a new journey and see the world through a different lens? Let me introduce you to the fabulous world of photography, where you can capture the beauty of everyday life and create lasting memories of your golden years.

Starting a photography project is an amazing way to rediscover your passion for life and unleash your creative potential. It's an opportunity to explore the world around you, meet new people, and learn new skills. Plus, it's a fantastic way to stay active and engaged in your community, making the most of your retirement.

Getting started is easy and doesn't require any fancy equipment. Start with the camera you already have – even a smartphone camera will do! The key is to focus on capturing the beauty in everyday moments: the warm smile of a stranger, the vibrant colors of a sunset, or the intricate patterns of a butterfly's wings.

Begin by setting a goal for your project, such as taking a photo every day for a year, or capturing the essence of your hometown in 100 images. This will give you a sense of purpose and direction as you embark on your creative journey. Don't worry about being a professional photographer; the goal is to have fun and document your unique perspective on life.

Next, explore different photography styles and techniques to find your personal style. Experiment with different angles, lighting, and subjects. Remember, there are no rules in photography – only opportunities to express yourself and tell your story.

Finally, share your work with friends, family, and fellow retirees. Create a photo album, start a blog, or even host a small exhibition. Sharing your work will not only inspire others but also give you a sense of accomplishment and pride.

Think of your photography project as a treasure hunt for the beauty hidden in everyday life. Just like a miner panning for gold, you'll sift through the ordinary to discover the extraordinary. And as you capture these precious moments, you'll realize that your best years are not behind you – they're right here, waiting for you to seize them with your lens. So, get out there, snap away, and remember: you're never too old to capture the magic of life. Happy shooting!

Bucket List # 52

Take an Art Class: Experiment with Different Mediums

"Creativity Takes Courage." – Henri Matisse –

Hello, my daring retirees! Are you ready to dive into a colorful world of self-expression and unleash your inner artist? Taking an art class is the perfect way to experiment with different mediums, learn new skills, and let your creativity shine.

Art is a powerful form of expression that allows you to explore your feelings, ideas, and dreams. It's not only therapeutic, but it's also a fantastic way to challenge yourself, stay mentally sharp, and meet like-minded individuals. Plus, it's never too late to tap into your artistic side – some of the greatest artists started their careers later in life.

To begin your artistic journey, research local art classes in your community. Many community centers, art galleries, and colleges offer classes for seniors in various mediums such as painting, drawing, pottery, or even digital art. Choose a medium that sparks your interest and sign up for a beginner's class.

Don't worry about having prior experience or being naturally talented. Art is about enjoying the process, experimenting, and learning as you go. Embrace the opportunity to try new techniques and find your unique style.

As you immerse yourself in the world of art, keep an open mind and be patient with yourself. Remember, every great artist started as a beginner. The more you practice and explore, the more your skills and confidence will grow.

Consider joining an art club or attending workshops to connect with fellow retirees who share your passion for creativity. You'll gain valuable insights, make new friends, and have the opportunity to collaborate on exciting projects.

Taking an art class is like stepping onto a roller coaster of color, texture, and imagination. You'll soar to new heights as you experiment with different mediums, and you'll find joy in the twists and turns of the creative process. The golden years are a time to rediscover your passions and let your inner artist shine.

Go ahead and pick up that paintbrush, molding clay, or sketchpad, and remember: your best years are right now, waiting to be painted with the vibrant colors of your unique artistic vision. Let the creativity flow.

Bucket List # 53

Learn to Knit or Crochet: Craft Your Own Creations

"The only thing better than a handmade item is the love and care that goes into making it." – Unknown –

Embrace a new hobby that allows you to create one-of-a-kind treasures with your own two hands. Learning to knit or crochet is a fantastic way to spend your golden years, creating beautiful and meaningful items for yourself and your loved ones.

Knitting and crocheting are not only enjoyable activities, but they also offer numerous benefits for your overall well-being. These crafts can help improve your dexterity, keep your mind sharp, and even reduce stress. Plus, they provide an opportunity to join social groups, make new friends, and share your creations with others.

To get started, all you need are some basic supplies like yarn, knitting needles or a crochet hook, and a beginner's guide or tutorial. Visit your local craft store or search online for beginner-friendly resources that will help you learn the basics of knitting or crocheting. Many libraries and community centers also offer free classes for retirees, which are a great way to get hands-on guidance and support.

As you begin your knitting or crocheting journey, start with simple projects like scarves, dishcloths, or hats. These smaller items will help you practice your new skills and build your confidence. Don't be afraid to make mistakes – every knitter and crocheter has a few wonky creations in their early days!

Once you've mastered the basics, you can explore more advanced techniques and patterns. Consider joining a knitting or crocheting group, either in-person or online, to connect with others who share your passion for crafting. You'll learn new tricks, gain inspiration, and make lasting friendships.

Learning to knit or crochet is like planting a seed in a garden of creativity. With time, patience, and care, your skills will grow and flourish, blossoming into a beautiful array of handmade creations. Your golden years are the perfect time to cultivate this garden, nurturing your talents and reaping the rewards of your efforts.

Grab your yarn and needles, and remember: these are the best years of your life, and they're just waiting for you to stitch together a beautiful tapestry of memories and accomplishments. Happy crafting!

Bucket List # 54

Attend a Storytelling Workshop: Share Your Life Experiences

"Storytelling reveals meaning without committing the error of defining it."

– Hannah Arendt –

Ready to weave a tapestry of memories and experiences that will inspire and entertain others. Attending a storytelling workshop is a delightful way to share your life experiences, learn the art of captivating an audience, and connect with others who have their own stories to tell.

Storytelling is an ancient art form that brings people together, fosters understanding, and allows us to share our unique perspectives. As a retiree, you have a wealth of life experiences and wisdom that others can learn from and enjoy. By attending a storytelling workshop, you'll gain the skills and confidence to share your tales, making a lasting impact on those who hear them.

To get started, look for storytelling workshops in your local community. Libraries, community centers, and even some theaters may offer classes or workshops for adults interested in learning the art of storytelling. You can also search online for virtual workshops, allowing you to learn from the comfort of your own home.

In a storytelling workshop, you'll learn techniques for crafting a compelling narrative, engaging your audience, and using your voice and body language to bring your stories to life. You'll also have the chance to practice your skills, receive feedback, and connect with others who share your passion for storytelling.

Once you've honed your storytelling abilities, consider sharing your tales with others in a variety of settings. You might volunteer to tell stories at local schools, libraries, or community events. You could even join a storytelling group or start your own, providing a platform for others to share their experiences as well.

Attending a storytelling workshop is like opening a treasure chest of memories and experiences. As you share your stories and listen to others, you'll discover a wealth of wisdom, laughter, and heartwarming moments. Your golden years are the perfect time to unlock this treasure and share it with the world.

Gather your stories, find a workshop, and remember: your best years are still unfolding, and every day brings a new opportunity to add another chapter to the amazing story of your life. Happy storytelling!

Bucket List # 55

Write a Letter to Your Future Self: Connect with Your Inner Wisdom

"The best way to predict the future is to create it." – Peter Drucker –

Writing a letter to your future self is a remarkable way to connect with your inner wisdom, set meaningful goals, and celebrate the growth and accomplishments you'll achieve in your golden years.

Writing a letter to your future self provides a unique opportunity to reflect on your life, explore your dreams and aspirations, and share advice and encouragement with the person you'll become. It's a powerful exercise in self-awareness and personal growth that can help you stay focused on what truly matters in life.

To get started, find a quiet space where you can relax and reflect on your life. Think about the experiences you've had, the lessons you've learned, and the person you want to become. Next, grab a pen and paper and start writing a letter to yourself, to be opened at a specific point in the future – perhaps five or ten years from now.

In your letter, share your thoughts on your current life, your hopes for the future, and any advice you'd like to give your future self. Be honest and open, expressing your feelings, concerns, and joys. You might also include details about your daily life, family, friends, and hobbies, creating a snapshot of your life at this moment in time.

Once you've finished your letter, seal it in an envelope and store it in a safe place, or use a website that will email your letter to you at a specified date in the future. When the time comes to open your letter, you'll be amazed at the wisdom, insight, and memories that you've shared with yourself.

Writing a letter to your future self is like planting a tree in the garden of your soul. As time passes, this tree will grow, its roots reaching deep into the rich soil of your experiences and its branches stretching towards the sky, bearing the fruits of wisdom, growth, and self-discovery. Your golden years are the perfect time to cultivate this garden, nurturing your dreams and aspirations for a fulfilling future.

So, pick up your pen, embrace your inner wisdom, and remember: your best years are still ahead, ripe with opportunity and adventure. Happy writing!

Bucket List # 56

Participate in an Open Mic Night: Share Your Creative Talents

"Use what talents you possess; the woods would be very silent if no birds sang there except those that sang best."
– Henry Van Dyke –

Ready to take center stage and share your creative gifts with the world. Participating in an open mic night is a fantastic opportunity to showcase your abilities, face your fears, and connect with others who share your passion for creativity and self-expression.

Open mic nights provide a welcoming and supportive environment for people of all ages and skill levels to perform and share their talents. Whether you're a singer, poet, comedian, or musician, there's a stage waiting for you to shine.

Taking part in an open mic night can help you build confidence, develop your skills, and make lasting connections with like-minded individuals. It's a wonderful way to challenge yourself and grow as a performer while enjoying the camaraderie and encouragement of your peers.

To get started, research open mic nights in your local area. Many cafes, bars, and community centers host regular events where anyone can sign up to perform. Check online listings, community bulletin boards, or social media groups for upcoming events, and don't be afraid to ask friends or acquaintances for recommendations.

When preparing for your open mic debut, choose a piece that showcases your unique talents and reflects your personality. Practice at home or in front of supportive friends or family members to gain confidence and polish your performance. Remember, it's not about being perfect – it's about sharing your passion and enjoying the experience.

On the night of your performance, arrive early to sign up and get a feel for the atmosphere. Take a deep breath, embrace your nerves, and remember that everyone in the audience is there to support and encourage you.

Participating in an open mic night is like diving into a pool of creativity, where each splash creates ripples of inspiration, laughter, and connection. Your golden years are the perfect time to take the plunge, immerse yourself in the vibrant waters of self-expression, and make a splash that will resonate with others.

Step up to the microphone, share your creative talents, and remember: your best years are still ahead, filled with adventure, discovery, and the sweet sound of applause. Break a leg!

Category 8: Culinary Adventures

Bucket List # 57

Host a Recipe Swap Party: Discover New Flavors

"Variety's the Very Spice of Life, that Gives it all its Flavor." – William Cowper –

Embarking on the journey of your golden years calls for trying new things and creating memories to cherish. One delightful way to spice up your retirement days is to host a recipe swap party. Not only will you discover new flavors, but you'll also strengthen friendships and create lasting bonds over shared culinary adventures.

Hosting a recipe swap party is an exciting opportunity to broaden your culinary horizons and explore different cuisines from around the world. By exchanging recipes with friends, you'll fill your cookbook with an array of scrumptious dishes that you can enjoy with your loved ones. This fun activity is a fantastic way to celebrate your retirement while embracing your love for cooking and trying something new.

To get started, pick a date, time, and location for your recipe swap party. You can choose to host it at your home or a local community center. Invite your friends, neighbors, and family members, and ask them to bring their favorite recipes along with a prepared dish to share.

On the day of the event, set up a welcoming space with tables for the dishes and recipe cards. Encourage your guests to mingle, sample each other's dishes, and share the stories behind their recipes. To make the event even more engaging, consider organizing a friendly competition by having guests vote on their favorite dish.

As the party comes to a close, have everyone exchange their recipe cards so they can take home a collection of new culinary delights to try in their own kitchens. You'll leave the party with a treasure trove of flavors and a newfound appreciation for the joy of cooking.

To sum it up, hosting a recipe swap party is like piecing together a beautiful quilt. Each patch represents a unique flavor, a cherished memory, and a loving friendship. With each stitch, you weave together a tapestry of experiences that will warm your heart and nourish your soul during your golden years.

Bucket List # 58

Take a Mixology Class: Craft Your Own Signature Cocktails

"You can't Pour from an Empty Cup. Take care of Yourself First." – Unknown –

As you explore on your next journey of your golden years, it's time to celebrate life to the fullest and add a dash of excitement to your everyday routine. One delightful way to do so is by taking a mixology class, where you'll learn to craft your very own signature cocktails. This fun-filled activity is perfect for those looking to explore their creative side, entertain guests, and enjoy a refreshing drink tailored to their tastes.

Taking a mixology class offers you the unique opportunity to acquire a new skill, make new friends, and become the life of any party. Imagine the joy of experimenting with various flavors, ingredients, and techniques to create the perfect cocktail that suits your personality. From classic drinks to innovative concoctions, the possibilities are endless!

So, how can you get started with mixology? Research local bars, restaurants, or adult education centers that offer mixology courses. Many of these classes cater to individuals of all skill levels, making it easy for you to jump right in and start crafting your own drinks. You can also look for online courses or instructional videos that can teach you the basics from the comfort of your own home.

Once you've honed your mixology skills, don't be afraid to host a cocktail party for your friends and family. Show off your newfound talents and invite your guests to sample your signature drinks. It's an excellent way to share your passion, create lasting memories, and make your retirement years all the more enjoyable.

In conclusion, taking a mixology class and crafting your own signature cocktails is like painting your masterpiece on the canvas of life. Each ingredient represents a color, a memory, and a cherished moment that you can share with others. As you mix and blend, you create a vibrant work of art that will bring joy and excitement to your golden years

Bucket List # 59

Attend a Chocolate or Cheese Tasting: Indulge Your Tastebuds

"Life is Short, Eat Dessert First." –Jacques Torres –

As you explore on the delightful journey of your golden years, it's time to treat yourself to the finer things in life. One such indulgence is attending a chocolate or cheese tasting event, where you can savor the rich, mouthwatering flavors and textures of these culinary delights. With each bite, you'll not only tantalize your taste buds but also create memories to cherish for years to come.

Attending a chocolate or cheese tasting offers a unique opportunity to explore the world of gourmet treats while expanding your palate. You'll learn about the history, production, and origins of these delicious products while savoring their exquisite flavors. In the company of fellow food enthusiasts, you can share stories, discuss flavor profiles, and perhaps even discover a newfound favorite.

To get started on this scrumptious adventure, research local chocolate or cheese shops, wineries, or gourmet food stores that host tasting events. Many of these venues offer guided tastings, allowing you to learn from experts and indulge in a truly unforgettable experience. Alternatively, consider hosting your own tasting party with friends, family, or neighbors. Simply ask each guest to bring a favorite chocolate or cheese.

Attending a chocolate or cheese tasting is more than just an indulgence – it's a celebration of life's simple pleasures. As you sample these delicious treats, you'll create moments of joy, laughter, and camaraderie with those around you.

In conclusion, attending a chocolate or cheese tasting is like embarking on a culinary treasure hunt. Each bite offers a unique flavor, a moment of discovery, and a shared experience with your fellow adventurers. As you explore the rich, delectable world of chocolate and cheese, let your golden years be filled with sweet indulgence and savory satisfaction. After all, life is too short not to enjoy the delicious treasures it has to offer.

Bucket List # 60

Learn the Art of Sushi Making: Roll Your Way to Deliciousness

"Life is Like Sushi you know it's Good when it's Fresh and Made with Love." – Unknown –

Your golden years are a time for exploration, growth, and embracing new experiences. One such delightful adventure is learning the art of sushi-making. This ancient culinary tradition is a beautiful blend of art, technique, and taste that will not only challenge your creativity but also provide you with delicious, healthy meals to share with your loved ones.

Learning to make sushi offers many benefits, such as promoting a healthy lifestyle, cultivating patience and precision, and providing a unique opportunity to bond with friends and family. Plus, you'll impress everyone with your newfound talent and enjoy mouthwatering sushi rolls crafted with your own hands.

To begin your sushi-making journey, look for local cooking schools, culinary studios, or even community centers that offer sushi-making classes. Many of these courses cater to beginners, ensuring that you'll feel comfortable and confident as you learn the basics. Alternatively, consider investing in a sushi-making kit and a reliable cookbook or online tutorial that can guide you through the process at home.

When learning to make sushi, you'll quickly discover that it's not just about the ingredients, but also about the presentation. Mastering the art of sushi-making will teach you to appreciate the beauty of each roll and the balance of flavors that make sushi such a beloved culinary delight.

In conclusion, learning the art of sushi-making is like learning a new dance. Each step, from selecting the freshest ingredients to carefully rolling and slicing each piece, is a graceful movement that comes together to create a stunning performance on your plate. As you embrace this culinary art form and weave it into the tapestry of your golden years, you'll find that your retirement is truly a time of delicious discovery, creativity, and joy. Remember, the best years of your life are still ahead, so embrace the adventure and savor every moment.

Bucket List # 61

Organize a Progressive Dinner Party: A Culinary Journey with Friends

"Food Tastes Better When you eat it with your Family and Friends." – Unknown –

Your golden years are a time for exploration, growth, and embracing new experiences. One such delightful adventure is learning the art of sushi-making. This ancient culinary tradition is a beautiful blend of art, technique, and taste that will not only challenge your creativity but also provide you with delicious, healthy meals to share with your loved ones.

Learning to make sushi offers many benefits, such as promoting a healthy lifestyle, cultivating patience and precision, and providing a unique opportunity to bond with friends and family. Plus, you'll impress everyone with your newfound talent and enjoy mouthwatering sushi rolls crafted with your own hands.

To begin your sushi-making journey, look for local cooking schools, culinary studios, or even community centers that offer sushi-making classes. Many of these courses cater to beginners, ensuring that you'll feel comfortable and confident as you learn the basics. Alternatively, consider investing in a sushi-making kit and a reliable cookbook or online tutorial that can guide you through the process at home.

When learning to make sushi, you'll quickly discover that it's not just about the ingredients, but also about the presentation. Mastering the art of sushi-making will teach you to appreciate the beauty of each roll and the balance of flavors that make sushi such a beloved culinary delight.

In conclusion, learning the art of sushi-making is like learning a new dance. Each step, from selecting the freshest ingredients to carefully rolling and slicing each piece, is a graceful movement that comes together to create a stunning performance on your plate. As you embrace this culinary art form and weave it into the tapestry of your golden years, you'll find that your retirement is truly a time of delicious discovery, creativity, and joy. Remember, the best years of your life are still ahead, so embrace the adventure and savor every moment.

Bucket List # 62

Take a Wine Appreciation Course: Savor the World's Finest Vintages

"Wine is One of the Most Civilized Things in the World and one of the most Natural things of the World that has been Brought to the Greatest Perfection." – Ernest Hemingway –

There's something magical about the world of wine – its rich history, the skill and artistry involved in its creation, and the pleasure of savoring a truly exquisite vintage. As you embrace the adventure of your golden years, consider delving into the fascinating realm of wine appreciation. Taking a wine appreciation course is a delightful way to enhance your knowledge, refine your palate, and open your senses to the world's finest vintages.

Enrolling in a wine appreciation course can offer several benefits during your retirement years. First, you'll gain valuable knowledge about different wine-producing regions, grape varieties, and wine-making techniques, transforming each sip into a journey of discovery. You'll also learn how to assess the quality of a wine, understand its unique characteristics, and pair it with the perfect dish – a skill that will undoubtedly impress your friends and family.

To get started, research local wine appreciation courses or workshops near you. Many wineries, wine shops, and educational institutions offer classes for beginners, making it easy to find one that suits your needs and interests. Additionally, consider joining a wine tasting club or attending wine-themed events to further immerse yourself in this captivating world.

As you explore on your wine appreciation journey, remember to savor the experience and share your newfound knowledge with others. Wine is best enjoyed in the company of friends, making it a perfect catalyst for creating memorable moments and fostering connections during your retirement years.

In conclusion, taking a wine appreciation course during your golden years is like unlocking a hidden treasure chest filled with the world's most exquisite gems. Each sip of wine unveils a new story, transporting you to faraway lands and immersing you in a rich tapestry of flavors and aromas. Embrace this journey with an open heart and an eager palate, and let your retirement years be filled with the joy, discovery, and enchantment that only the world of wine can offer.

Bucket List # 63

Create Your Own Spice Blends: Unlock the Secrets of Flavor

"Variety's the Very Spice of life that Gives it all its Flavor." – William Cowper –

As you embark on the exciting journey of your golden years, consider adding a pinch of flavor to your life by creating your own spice blends. This fun and rewarding endeavor not only allows you to experiment with new taste sensations but also offers a unique opportunity to share your culinary creations with friends and loved ones.

Creating your own spice blends has numerous benefits. Firstly, it empowers you to control the flavors and quality of your dishes, ensuring that each meal is seasoned to perfection. Secondly, it's an economical and eco-friendly alternative to store-bought blends, as you can buy spices in bulk and reduce packaging waste. Lastly, homemade spice blends make for thoughtful and personalized gifts that are sure to delight the taste buds of your friends and family.

To get started on your spice blending adventure, begin by researching popular spice combinations from different cuisines around the world. This will help you understand the fundamentals of flavor pairings and inspire you to create your own unique concoctions. Next, stock your pantry with a variety of high-quality, whole spices that can be easily ground and mixed to create your blends.

As you share your spice blends with friends and family, remember that the joy of this endeavor lies not only in the flavors themselves but also in the connections and memories you create. Savor the moments spent crafting and enjoying your culinary creations, and let the warmth of shared experiences fill your golden years with zest and delight.

In conclusion, creating your own spice blends during your retirement years is like painting with a vibrant palette of flavors. Each spice blend you create adds a new hue to the canvas of your life, infusing it with richness, depth, and a sense of adventure. Embrace this flavorful journey with an open heart and a curious mind, and let your golden years be filled with the joy, creativity, and enchantment that come from unlocking the secrets of flavor.

Bucket List # 64

Attend a Food Festival: Celebrate the Joy of Cuisine

"People Who Love to Eat are Always the Best People." – Julia Child –

As you explore the excitement and adventure of your golden years, consider adding a dash of culinary delight to your life by attending food festivals. These gastronomic gatherings celebrate the joy of cuisine and offer a unique opportunity to sample mouthwatering dishes from around the world while connecting with fellow food enthusiasts.

Attending food festivals has several benefits. Firstly, it broadens your culinary horizons, allowing you to discover new flavors, ingredients, and cooking techniques. This newfound knowledge can inspire you to experiment in your own kitchen, elevating your home-cooked meals to new heights. Secondly, food festivals provide a vibrant atmosphere that fosters a sense of community and camaraderie among attendees, creating lasting memories and friendships.

To get started on your food festival adventure, begin by researching local and regional events that showcase various types of cuisine. You may be surprised to find a diverse array of festivals right in your backyard, offering an abundance of opportunities to indulge your taste buds and expand your culinary knowledge. As you gain confidence and experience, consider attending larger, more renowned food festivals around the world, transforming your passion for food into a global adventure.

As you explore the world of food festivals, remember that the heart of this experience lies not only in the dishes themselves but also in the connections and memories you create. Share your love for food with friends and family by inviting them to join you at these events or even starting your own food-themed gatherings.

In conclusion, attending food festivals during your golden years is like embarking on a culinary treasure hunt, with each event unveiling a cornucopia of tantalizing flavors and experiences. Embrace this gastronomic journey with an open heart and a curious palate, and let your retirement years be filled with the joy, wonder, and connection that only the world of cuisine can provide.

Category 9: Embracing Your Inner Child

Bucket List # 65

Join a Hula Hoop Group: Spin Your Way to Fun

"Age is an Issue of Mind over Matter. If you Don't Mind, it doesn't Matter."

– Mark Twain –

Get ready to spin your way to fun as you join a hula hoop group! Hula hooping is not just for kids; it's a fantastic way for retirees to stay active, socialize, and have a blast. The best part is, it's easy to learn, and you don't need any prior experience.

Why is joining a hula hoop group important for retirees? For starters, it's a fantastic way to stay physically fit. Hooping can improve your balance, flexibility, and core strength. Plus, it's a low-impact exercise, making it perfect for those with joint concerns or mobility issues.

But hula hooping isn't just about the physical benefits. It's also a great opportunity to make new friends and create lasting connections. Hula hoop groups attract people of all ages and backgrounds, so you'll have a chance to share laughter, stories, and encouragement with others who are just as excited about this fun-filled activity as you are.

Here's how you can get started:

- **Find a group**: Search online or check local community centers, gyms, or parks for hula hoop groups in your area.
- **Get the right hoop**: Adult hula hoops are larger and heavier than those made for kids. Look for one with a diameter of around 40 inches and a weight of 1 to 2 pounds.
- **Learn the basics:** There are plenty of online tutorials and videos available to help you learn the fundamentals of hula hooping.

Have fun: The most important thing is to enjoy yourself. Hula hooping is all about having a good time, so let loose, laugh, and enjoy the company of your fellow hoopers.

Imagine your golden years as a garden filled with vibrant flowers. Joining a hula hoop group is like planting a bright, joyful bloom in the center of your garden, adding color and excitement to your days.

Bucket List # 66

Attend a Laughter Workshop: Rediscover the Joy of Laughter

"Laughter is the Sun that Drives winter from the Human Face." – Victor Hugo –

Let the sunshine in and rediscover the joy of laughter by attending a laughter workshop. These fun-filled sessions are designed to help you unleash your inner comedian, brighten your spirits, and even improve your health. Why not give it a try? After all, laughter is the best medicine, and your golden years deserve to be filled with happiness and joy.

Why should you attend a laughter workshop? For starters, laughter has countless health benefits. It can help lower stress, boost your immune system, and even improve your heart health. Besides, sharing a hearty laugh with others is an excellent way to create connections, make new friends, and strengthen bonds with loved ones.

Here's how you can get started on your laughter-filled journey:

- **Find a workshop**: Look for laughter workshops in your local area by searching online, checking with community centers, or asking friends and family for recommendations.
- **Keep an open mind**: Laughter workshops often involve silly exercises and games to help you tap into your playful side. Embrace the experience and don't be afraid to let loose.
- **Dress comfortably**: You'll likely be moving around and engaging in various activities during the workshop, so wear clothes that allow you to move freely and comfortably.
- **Spread the laughter:** After attending a workshop, share your newfound laughter skills with others. Organize a laughter club with friends, or simply take the time to share a joke with someone who could use a smile.

Think of your retirement years as a warm, sunny day. Attending a laughter workshop is like inviting a cool, refreshing breeze into your life, lifting your spirits and bringing joy to those around you. Go ahead and let laughter fill your heart and brighten your golden years – after all, these are the best years of your life.

Bucket List # 67

Try Adult Coloring: Unwind with Color and Creativity

"Creativity is Intelligence Having Fun." – Albert Einstein
–

Unleash your inner artist and unwind with color and creativity by trying adult coloring! This enjoyable activity isn't just for kids; it's an excellent way for people of all ages to relax, express themselves, and even boost their mental well-being. Your golden years are the perfect time to explore new hobbies and embrace the joy of creativity.

Why is adult coloring important for retirees? For starters, it's a fantastic way to relax and reduce stress. Focusing on intricate designs and vibrant colors can help calm your mind and provide a soothing escape from everyday worries. Plus, coloring can stimulate your brain, improve your focus, and even enhance your fine motor skills.

Ready to add a splash of color to your life? Here's how to get started:

- **Choose your materials**: Adult coloring books come in various themes and styles, from intricate mandalas to whimsical animals. Pick a book that speaks to you and don't forget to grab some coloring tools, like colored pencils or markers.

- **Find a comfortable spot:** Set up a cozy space where you can color in peace. This could be a quiet corner of your home or even a sunny spot in your backyard.
- **Start with simple designs**: If you're new to adult coloring, begin with less complicated images to build your confidence and get used to the process. As you become more comfortable, you can move on to more intricate designs.

Make it social: Invite friends or family members to join you for a coloring session. This is a great way to bond, share ideas, and have fun together.

Imagine your retirement years as a blank canvas, waiting for you to add your unique touch. Trying adult coloring is like picking up a paintbrush and filling your canvas with vibrant colors, patterns, and textures. Explore, your creative side and let the colors flow.

Bucket List # 68

Host a Retro Game Night: Relive the Fun of Yesteryears

"We Don't Stop laying because We grow old; We Grow Old because we Stop Playing."

– George Bernard Shaw –

Ready to relive the fun of yesteryears by hosting a retro game night. This blast from the past is not only a delightful way to spend an evening but also a fantastic opportunity to reconnect with friends, share laughter, and create lasting memories. Dust off those old board games, shuffle the cards, and let the games begin.

Why is hosting a retro game night important for retirees? For starters, it's a great way to rekindle the joy of simple, screen-free entertainment. Playing board games, card games, and other nostalgic favorites can also stimulate your mind, improve your memory, and promote social interaction.

Eager to host your own retro game night? Here's how to get started:

- **Gather your games:** Dig through your attic or basement to find classic games from your youth. Think Monopoly,

Scrabble, Clue, or even a deck of cards. If you don't have any games on hand, consider visiting thrift stores, garage sales, or searching online for retro gems.

- **Invite your guests**: Reach out to friends, family, and neighbors to join in on the fun. Encourage everyone to bring a favorite game from their past to share with the group.
- **Set the scene:** Transform your living room into a cozy game haven by arranging comfortable seating, setting out tasty snacks, and creating a warm, inviting atmosphere.
- **Enjoy the memories:** As you play, take the time to reminisce about the good old days and share stories from your past. This is a wonderful way to strengthen bonds and create new memories together.

Think of your golden years as a treasure chest, filled with precious gems of memories and experiences. Hosting a retro game night is like adding a sparkling jewel to your collection, one that shines with laughter, friendship, and the warmth of shared history. Roll the dice, and let the fun begin – these are the best years of your life.

Bucket List # 69

Organize a Costume Party: Dress Up and Let Loose

"Life is like a Costume Party, Enjoy Dressing up and Playing a Part." – Unknown –

Do you ever miss the days when you could let your hair down and have some carefree fun? Well, there's no better time than now to bring back that youthful spirit! Organizing a costume party is a fantastic way to relive those precious moments and create new memories with your loved ones during your golden years.

A costume party is an event where everyone dresses up as a character, an object, or a theme. The beauty of it is that you can be anything or anyone you want to be, even if it's just for a night. Hosting a costume party is a great way to bond with old friends and make new ones, while also allowing your creative juices to flow.

To get started, choose a theme that you and your friends will enjoy. It could be as simple as your favorite decade, TV show, or movie, or as unique as a "come as your favorite quote" theme. Once you've settled on a theme, plan the decorations, food, and music that will accompany it. Send out invitations with clear instructions on the dress code, so everyone knows what's expected.

Don't be afraid to go all out with your costume, and encourage your guests to do the same. You can even hold a contest for the best outfit, with prizes for the winners. To make the night even more memorable, consider setting up a photo booth with fun props, so everyone can take pictures and have a keepsake of the event.

In conclusion, hosting a costume party is like opening a treasure chest filled with joy, laughter, and adventure. It's a chance to express yourself, connect with others, and rediscover the fun side of life. Remember, your golden years are here to be enjoyed to the fullest, so take this opportunity to dress up, let loose, and make the most of the best years ahead.

Bucket List # 70

Go on a Playground Adventure: Play Like No One's Watching

"Growing Old is Mandatory, but Growing up is Optional." – Walt Disney –

Explore your inner child and experience the joy of being carefree by going on a playground adventure. Play like no one's watching and enjoy the simple pleasure of swinging on swings, sliding down slides, and climbing on jungle gyms. Not only will you have fun, but you'll also improve your physical and mental well-being.

The importance of playtime should never be underestimated, even in our golden years. Playing on a playground helps keep your mind sharp, your body fit, and your spirit lifted. Swinging on swings, for example, can help improve your balance and coordination, while climbing and stretching can increase your flexibility and strength.

To begin your playground adventure, locate a nearby park or playground that offers a variety of equipment for all ages. If you're unsure where to find one, a simple internet search or asking locals should point you in the right direction. When you arrive at the playground, take a moment to observe the different play structures and choose one that you feel comfortable with and excited to try.

Don't worry about what others may think; remember, you're there to have fun and enjoy yourself. You can invite friends or family members to join you or even make new friends while you're there.

As you play, pay attention to your body and its limitations. It's essential to stay safe and know when to take breaks or slow down. Don't push yourself too hard, but don't be afraid to challenge yourself either. Playtime is all about finding the perfect balance.

To sum it up, going on a playground adventure is like rediscovering the fountain of youth hidden within yourself. It's a chance to break free from the constraints of adulthood and experience the pure, unadulterated joy of play once more. Seize this opportunity to laugh, have fun, and make the most of your best years ahead.

Bucket List # 71

Build a Fort: Ignite Your Imagination and Sense of Wonder

"The World is but a Canvas to our Imagination." – Henry David Thoreau –

Remember the days when you could spend hours building forts out of blankets, pillows, and furniture? It's time to bring back that sense of wonder and ignite your imagination by building a fort once again. This creative activity will not only transport you back to the carefree days of childhood but also provide a unique bonding experience with friends and family.

Building a fort is an excellent way to tap into your creativity, problem-solving skills, and resourcefulness. It's a reminder that even in our golden years, we can still have fun and explore new experiences. Plus, it's a great way to share stories, laughter, and cherished memories with your loved ones.

To get started, gather materials that can be used to construct your fort. You can use blankets, sheets, pillows, chairs, and anything else you have on hand. Don't be afraid to think outside the box and repurpose items from around your home. Once you have your supplies, choose a location for your fort, such as your living room, backyard, or even a local park.

Next, enlist the help of friends or family members who are up for the challenge. Share your ideas and work together to create a fort that embodies your combined creativity and sense of adventure. Remember, there's no right or wrong way to build a fort, so let your imagination run wild!

When your fort is complete, take a moment to step back and admire your handiwork. Then, crawl inside and enjoy the fruits of your labor. Share stories, play games, or simply relax and bask in the cozy atmosphere you've created together.

In conclusion, building a fort is like constructing a magical portal to your youth. It's an opportunity to reconnect with your inner child and experience the joy, wonder, and imagination that comes from creating something out of nothing.

Bucket List # 72

Try a Trampoline Workout: Bounce Your Way to Fitness

"Age is no Barrier. It's a Limitation you Put on your Mind." – Jackie Joyner-Kersee –

It's time to relive that thrill and bounce your way to fitness with a trampoline workout. This exciting and unique form of exercise is not only fun but also offers numerous health benefits, making it the perfect addition to your golden years.

A trampoline workout is an effective way to improve cardiovascular health, increase muscle strength, enhance balance, and promote overall well-being. Plus, it's low-impact, which makes it an ideal exercise option for people of all ages and fitness levels, especially those in their golden years.

To get started, first, find a local trampoline park or gym that offers trampoline fitness classes. You can also purchase a small, personal-sized trampoline (also known as a rebounder) for at-home workouts. Remember, safety comes first, so make sure you're using appropriate equipment and following the recommended guidelines.

Learn some basic trampoline exercises, such as jumping jacks, high knees, and gentle bounces. You can find instructional videos online or join a class to learn proper techniques and form. As you become more comfortable and confident, you can progress to more advanced moves and even incorporate weights or resistance bands into your routine.

Invite friends or family members to join you in your trampoline workouts for added fun and motivation. Exercising together not only strengthens your body but also strengthens your relationships and social connections. A trampoline workout is a unique and exhilarating way to do just that, allowing you to bounce, laugh, and play your way to a healthier and happier life.

In conclusion, trying a trampoline workout is like rediscovering the spring in your step that you thought was lost to the sands of time. It's an opportunity to reclaim your zest for life, improve your health, and have a blast while doing it. Embrace the bounce, and let your trampoline workout propel you into the best years ahead.

Category 10: Giving Back and Making a Difference

Bucket List # 73

Volunteer at a Local Nonprofit: Share Your Skills and Wisdom

"Service to others is the Rent you Pay for your Room here on Earth." – Muhammad Ali –

Volunteering at a local nonprofit is a fantastic way to share your skills, wisdom, and experience with others while connecting with your community. Not only will you be making a difference in the lives of those around you, but you'll also discover the joy and fulfillment that comes from giving back.

Volunteering is important because it allows you to contribute to the greater good, support causes close to your heart, and create lasting connections with like-minded individuals. Furthermore, it can improve your mental and emotional well-being by giving you a sense of purpose, accomplishment, and belonging.

To get started, first, identify your passions, interests, and skills. What causes are you passionate about? Which skills and experiences do you have that could benefit a nonprofit organization? Once you have a clear idea, research local nonprofits or community organizations that align with your interests and values.

Next, reach out to the organization of your choice and inquire about volunteer opportunities. Many nonprofits are eager to have volunteers with diverse skill sets and life experiences, so don't hesitate to offer your unique talents and expertise. You can also attend local volunteer fairs or use online resources to find opportunities that match your criteria. Embrace the challenges and rewards that come with serving others, and treasure the relationships you build along the way.

In conclusion, volunteering at a local nonprofit is like planting seeds of kindness and compassion that will grow and flourish for years to come. It's an opportunity to leave a lasting legacy while enriching your own life and the lives of those around you. Local nonprofit is like casting a pebble into a pond, creating ripples that spread far and wide. Your acts of kindness and generosity have the power to inspire and uplift countless lives, creating a legacy that will endure long after your time as a volunteer.

Bucket List # 74

Mentor a Young Person: Inspire the Next Generation

"Children are the Living Messages we Send to a Time we will not See." – Neil Postman –

Mentoring a young person is an extraordinary opportunity to share your wisdom, experience, and life lessons with someone just beginning their journey. As a mentor, you can help shape the character and aspirations of a young individual, fostering their growth and empowering them to reach their full potential.

Mentoring is important because it provides young people with guidance, encouragement, and support, helping them navigate the challenges of life with greater confidence and resilience. As a mentor, you can be a role model and a source of inspiration, nurturing the dreams and aspirations of the next generation.

To get started, identify your areas of expertise and interests. What valuable lessons and experiences have you gained throughout your life that you could share with a young person? Once you have a clear idea, research mentoring programs in your area, such as schools, community centers, or nonprofit organizations that focus on youth development.

Next, reach out to the mentoring program of your choice and express your interest in becoming a mentor. They will guide you through the process, which may include an application, background check, and training. Once you're matched with a mentee, take the time to get to know them and build a strong relationship based on trust, respect, and understanding.

As a mentor, remember to be patient, compassionate, and supportive. Be prepared to listen, share your experiences, and offer guidance when needed. Encourage your mentee to dream big, set goals, and work towards achieving them. Your guidance and support will help them grow into confident, capable adults.

In conclusion, mentoring a young person is like nurturing a delicate flower. With patience, love, and care, you can help them blossom into their full potential and beauty. By sharing your wisdom, experience, and guidance, you are making a lasting impact on the lives of future generations and enriching your own golden years. Embrace the opportunity to inspire the next generation, and let the joy and satisfaction of making a difference brighten your best years ahead.

Bucket List # 75

Participate in Community Service Projects: Create a Positive Impact

"Small Acts, when Multiplied by Millions of People, can Transform the World."

– Howard Zinn –

Participating in community service projects is an excellent way to create a positive impact while connecting with your neighbors and enjoying your golden years. By joining forces with others, you can help make your community a better place to live for everyone.

Community service projects are important because they foster a sense of unity, promote social responsibility, and address various local needs. By working together, you and your fellow volunteers can accomplish incredible things and improve the lives of those around you.

To get started, look for community service projects in your area that align with your interests and passions. Local organizations like schools, libraries, parks, and shelters often host service events and initiatives that you can join. You can also connect with local clubs or social groups that organize regular service activities.

Next, reach out to the project organizers and sign up as a volunteer. Be sure to ask about any specific skills or resources they may need, and offer your unique talents and expertise. Don't hesitate to invite friends and family members to join you, as working together on a common goal can strengthen your relationships and make the experience even more rewarding.

As you participate in community service projects, be open to learning from others and embrace the opportunity to grow. Each project will present its own set of challenges and rewards, but the satisfaction of knowing that you're making a difference will make the journey worthwhile.

In conclusion, participating in community service projects is like weaving a beautiful tapestry of kindness, compassion, and cooperation. Each volunteer contributes their own unique thread, and together, you create a masterpiece that enriches the lives of everyone in your community. Embrace this opportunity to make a positive impact and cherish the memories, friendships, and personal growth that come with it.

Bucket List # 76

Support a Cause Close to Your Heart: Make a Difference in the World

"Never Doubt that a Small Group of Thoughtful, committed Citizens can change the World; indeed, it's the only thing that ever has." – Margaret Mead –

Your golden years are the perfect time to dedicate your time, energy, and resources to a cause that truly matters to you. By championing a meaningful issue, you can make a lasting impact on the lives of others and create a legacy of compassion and positive change.

Supporting a cause is important because it allows you to use your unique skills, passions, and experiences to address pressing issues in the world. Your dedication can inspire others to join you in making a difference, and together, you can create a powerful force for good.

To get started, first identify a cause that truly resonates with you. This could be anything from environmental conservation to education, healthcare, or social justice. Reflect on your personal experiences, values, and interests to find a cause that aligns with your passion.

Next, research organizations, charities, or community groups that work on your chosen cause. Learn about their missions, goals, and the ways in which they make a difference. Once you've found an organization that aligns with your values, explore the different ways you can support their efforts. This may include volunteering, fundraising, advocating, or sharing your expertise and skills.

As you support your chosen cause, be prepared to invest your time and energy wholeheartedly. Stay informed about the issues, attend events, and engage with like-minded individuals who share your passion. By connecting with others, you can create a network of support that strengthens your efforts and amplifies your impact.

In conclusion, supporting a cause close to your heart is like lighting a candle in the darkness. Your dedication and commitment can ignite a flame of hope, compassion, and positive change that illuminates the world. Experience this opportunity to make a difference in your golden years and let the warmth of your actions brighten the best years ahead.

Bucket List # 77

Become a Foster Grandparent: Share Your Love and Support

"The Love of a Grandparent for his/her Grandchild is like no other. It Plays a part in the heart that Even time Cannot Erase." – Unknown –

Sharing your love, support, and wisdom with a child in need, you can create a lasting bond that enriches both your life and theirs. Embrace the opportunity to make a positive impact on a young person's life and let the joy of nurturing and guiding a child brighten your golden years.

Becoming a foster grandparent is important because it offers children the stability, care, and encouragement they need to thrive. Your presence can provide them with a sense of belonging, and the life lessons you share can help shape their future.

To get started, research local organizations and programs that connect foster grandparents with children in need. These programs often provide training and support to help you navigate your new role. Reach out to the program coordinator, and express your interest in becoming a foster grandparent.

Once you're connected with a child, be prepared to invest your time, energy, and love into building a strong, nurturing relationship. Take the time to get to know the child, their interests, and their needs. Be patient, understanding, and compassionate, and let your heart guide you as you support and encourage them in their journey.

As a foster grandparent, you have the unique opportunity to serve as a mentor, confidant, and friend to a child in need. Your love and support can create a sense of stability and belonging that helps them navigate life's challenges with resilience and confidence.

In conclusion, becoming a foster grandparent is like planting a seed of love and nurturing it into a beautiful, thriving tree. Your love, support, and guidance can provide the strong roots and branches that help a child grow into their fullest potential. Embrace this opportunity to make a difference in a young person's life, and let the joy and satisfaction of your role as a foster grandparent illuminate the best years ahead.

Bucket List # 78

Teach a Class in Your Area of Expertise: Share Your Knowledge

"Share your Knowledge. It is a way to Achieve Immortality." – Dalai Lama –

Teaching is not only about imparting knowledge but also about growing alongside your students. Embrace the opportunity to learn from them, as they may offer fresh perspectives and insights that can enrich your own understanding of the subject. Teaching a class in your area of expertise is a fantastic way to give back to your community, engage with others, and keep your mind sharp during your golden years.

Teaching is important because it allows you to pass on your valuable skills and insights to a new generation. By sharing your knowledge, you can inspire others to explore their interests, ignite their passions, and build their own expertise. Moreover, teaching is a rewarding experience that can enrich your life with a sense of purpose and fulfillment.

To get started, identify a subject you are passionate about and feel confident teaching. This could be anything from painting or cooking to gardening or woodworking. Next, research local community centers, libraries, or schools that may be interested in hosting your class. Reach out to these organizations and propose your idea, highlighting your expertise and the potential benefits of your class.

Once you have secured a venue, plan your curriculum and gather any necessary materials. Be sure to structure your class in a way that is engaging, informative, and accessible to students of varying skill levels. Promote your class through local bulletin boards, social media, or word of mouth, and be prepared to adapt your teaching style to accommodate the unique needs and interests of your students.

In conclusion, teaching a class in your area of expertise is like lighting a candle in the darkness. Your knowledge, experience, and passion can ignite a spark within your students, illuminating their path toward growth and discovery. Embrace this opportunity to share your wisdom and make a lasting impact on the lives of others, and let the joy and satisfaction of teaching brighten the best years ahead.

Bucket List # 79

Organize a Fundraiser: Bring People Together for a Good Cause

"Act as if What you do makes a Difference. It does." – William James –

Retirement is a wonderful time to give back to your community and make a meaningful impact on the lives of others. One exciting way to do this is by organizing a fundraiser to bring people together for a good cause. By hosting a charity event, you can help support a cause close to your heart, while also fostering a sense of unity and camaraderie among your friends, family, and neighbors.

Organizing a fundraiser is important because it raises awareness and generates much-needed funds for a deserving organization. Additionally, it can strengthen your connections with others, as you work together toward a common goal, and create lasting memories in the process.

To get started, first choose a cause or organization you feel passionate about. Research local or international charities that align with your values, and contact them to express your interest in organizing a fundraiser on their behalf.

Once you have selected your event, gather a team of volunteers to help with planning and organizing. Assign tasks such as securing a venue, marketing the event, and arranging entertainment or refreshments. Create a timeline to keep everyone on track and ensure that all details are in place well before the big day.

On the day of the event, make sure everyone is prepared and ready to go. Encourage your team to have fun and engage with attendees, creating a welcoming and inclusive atmosphere. After the event, remember to thank all those who participated and share the results of the fundraiser with the community.

In conclusion, organizing a fundraiser is like weaving a beautiful tapestry. Each thread represents the time, effort, and passion of those involved, and when brought together, they create a vibrant and meaningful masterpiece. Explore the opportunity to make a difference in the world and let this experience add color and joy to your golden years.

Bucket List # 80

Advocate for Change: Use Your Voice for the Greater Good

"Never Doubt that a Small Group of Thoughtful, Committed Citizens can change the world; indeed, it's the Only thing that ever has." – Margaret Mead –

Retirement is a wonderful time to explore new passions and make a difference in the world around you. One way to create a positive impact is by advocating for change and using your voice to support causes that matter to you. Advocacy is important because it helps raise awareness about important issues, drives positive change, and empowers others to get involved.

To begin advocating for change, start by identifying an issue or cause you're passionate about. This could be anything from environmental conservation, social justice, or education reform to supporting local community initiatives. Research the topic to better understand the current challenges and potential solutions. This will provide you with the knowledge and confidence to speak up and take action.

Next, seek out organizations or groups that align with your chosen cause. Reach out to them and inquire about ways you can get involved, whether it's through volunteering, fundraising, or attending events. Building connections with like-minded individuals can be a powerful motivator and provide you with valuable support and resources.

Celebrate the milestones and successes along the way, no matter how small they may seem. Acknowledge the difference your advocacy has made and use it to fuel your passion for creating a better world.

In summary, advocating for change during your golden years is like lighting a series of candles in the darkness. Each small flame represents the positive impact you have on the lives of others and the world at large. As more and more candles are lit, the darkness begins to recede, and the world becomes a brighter, more compassionate place. Embrace this opportunity to illuminate the world with your passion and dedication, and let it fill your retirement with meaning and fulfillment.

Category II: Rediscovering Your Hometown

Bucket List # 81

Take a Guided Walking Tour: Unearth Local History and Secrets

"Life is like a Walking Tour, the more you Explore, the Richer your journey becomes."

– Unknown –

Taking a guided walking tour is a fantastic way to unearth local history and secrets while enjoying your retirement years. These tours offer an opportunity to learn about the rich tapestry of stories and events that have shaped the places you visit, all while getting some fresh air and exercise.

To get started, research walking tours in your local area or the next city you plan to visit. Many towns and cities have a variety of guided tours available, ranging from historical walks to foodie adventures. Look for tours that match your interests and physical capabilities. Tours can be found through local tourism boards, online resources, or word of mouth.

Once you have chosen your tour, make sure you wear comfortable walking shoes, dress appropriately for the weather, and bring essentials like water, sunscreen, and a hat. Don't forget your camera or smartphone to capture memorable moments and sights during the tour.

On the tour, be open to asking questions and engaging with your tour guide. They are a wealth of knowledge and often have fascinating anecdotes to share. Listen to their stories and absorb the unique insights they provide into the local culture and history.

Taking a guided walking tour is not only a fun way to spend your day but also an opportunity to make new friends. Chat with your fellow tour-goers and bond over your shared interests and discoveries.

In conclusion, taking guided walking tours and embracing new experiences is like planting a garden of memories in your golden years. Each tour represents a seed, and with each step, you nurture and grow your garden, filling it with the vibrant colors of life. As you continue to explore and learn, your garden will flourish, reflecting the richness and joy of your retirement journey.

Bucket List # 82

Attend a Community Event: Connect with Your Neighbors

"Alone, we can do so Little; Together, we can do so Much."
– Helen Keller –

Retirement provides an excellent opportunity to strengthen your bonds within your community and create lasting connections with your neighbors. Attending community events not only adds excitement to your life but also allows you to make new friends, engage with your surroundings, and contribute to the vibrant tapestry of your local area.

To get started, check out your local newspaper, community bulletin board, or online forums to find out about upcoming events. These can range from art exhibitions, farmers' markets, and outdoor concerts to local sports games, charity fundraisers, or holiday celebrations. Choose events that interest you and align with your passions or hobbies.

When attending these events, be open to meeting new people and starting conversations. Remember, many others are also looking to make new connections and share their stories. Be curious, ask questions, and listen attentively – you might discover new interests or uncover hidden talents among your neighbors.

Volunteering at community events is another way to get involved and contribute to your local area. By offering your time and skills, you can help create a positive and welcoming atmosphere for everyone. Moreover, volunteering is an excellent way to make a difference in the lives of others while also enriching your own.

Experience community events in your retirement is like weaving a beautiful, colorful quilt. Each event represents a unique thread, and as you attend more gatherings and meet new people, these threads intertwine to form a warm and comforting blanket. This quilt not only represents the connections you've made but also serves as a reminder that your golden years are filled with love, laughter, and shared experiences, making your life richer and more fulfilling. By embracing these opportunities, you'll create a fulfilling and memorable chapter in your life, one that you can cherish and celebrate for years to come.

Bucket List # 83

Explore Local Museums and Galleries: Discover Hidden Treasures

"Art enables us to Find Ourselves and lose Ourselves at the Same Time."

– Thomas Merton –

Retirement is the perfect time to immerse yourself in the world of art and history by exploring local museums and galleries. These cultural institutions offer a treasure trove of hidden gems, waiting to be discovered by curious minds like yours.

To start your journey, make a list of museums and galleries in your area. Consider visiting a variety of institutions, from renowned museums to smaller, specialized galleries. Each one has its own unique collection and story to share, offering you a rich tapestry of experiences.

When you arrive, take your time to explore each exhibit. Allow yourself to be captivated by the stories behind the artifacts, artworks, and historical events. Don't be afraid to ask questions or join guided tours, as these can provide valuable insights and enhance your understanding of the displays.

As you delve deeper into these cultural spaces, you'll begin to see the world from new perspectives. This can ignite your creativity, fuel your curiosity, and help you gain a deeper appreciation for the beauty and diversity of human expression. Plus, visiting museums and galleries can be a great way to socialize with like-minded individuals who share your passion for art and history.

Exploring museums and galleries is like embarking on a thrilling treasure hunt. Each room reveals a new trove of artifacts, transporting you to different eras and cultures. As you wander through these hallowed halls, you'll uncover priceless gems that will enrich your mind and soul, reminding you that your golden years are a canvas filled with endless opportunities for discovery and growth. By stopping to admire each one, you'll not only create lasting memories but also nourish your soul with the rich tapestry of human history and expression. Embrace this opportunity to rediscover the world and savor the best years of your life, filled with art, adventure, and unending wonder.

Bucket List # 84

Try a New Local Restaurant or Café: Savor Your Town's Culinary Delights

"Life is a Combination of Magic and Pasta." – Federico Fellini –

As you embark on your golden years, remember that variety is the spice of life. Trying new local restaurants and cafes is a delicious way to experience new flavors, cultures, and atmospheres right in your hometown. You might just discover a new favorite dish, or maybe even a new favorite spot to spend time with friends and family.

Begin by making a list of the eateries you've always been curious about, or ask for recommendations from friends, family, and neighbors. Plan a weekly or monthly outing to explore these culinary destinations. Don't be afraid to venture outside your comfort zone, as you never know what gastronomic delights might be waiting just around the corner.

When visiting a new restaurant or café, take the time to chat with the staff and learn about their culinary inspirations, locally sourced ingredients, or even their personal stories. You might be surprised at the connections you can make through a shared love of food.

Trying new local restaurants and cafes can also be a fantastic way to support small businesses in your community. As you enjoy their culinary creations, you are helping to foster a thriving local economy and encouraging the growth of unique dining experiences in your town.

Consider your culinary explorations as a voyage through a vast ocean of flavors. Each new restaurant or café is like an uncharted island, offering hidden treasures just waiting to be discovered. With each new dining experience, you'll create lasting memories, forge connections with your community, and delight your taste buds in ways you never thought possible. Dive into this flavorful adventure and let your golden years be filled with the joy of delicious discoveries. In doing so, you will be cultivating a rich and fulfilling life during your golden years, creating a tapestry of flavors and memories that will last a lifetime.

Bucket List # 85

Attend a Local Theater Production: Support the Arts in Your Community

"Art is Not what you see, but What you make Others See."
– Edgar Degas –

There's nothing quite like the magic of live theater to transport you to new worlds and bring stories to life. As you embark on your journey of retirement adventures, attending a local theater production is a fantastic way to support the arts in your community and enjoy an unforgettable experience.

Theater is a vital part of any community, fostering creativity, collaboration, and a sense of belonging among its participants and audiences. By attending local productions, you're not only showing your support for the artists, but you're also contributing to the vibrancy and cultural richness of your town or city.

Getting started is easy. Keep an eye out for advertisements in local newspapers or on social media for upcoming productions. Many theaters also have websites where you can sign up for newsletters to stay informed about their latest shows. Another great idea is to join a theater group or club, where you can meet like-minded people who share your passion for the stage.

When attending a production, don't be afraid to step out of your comfort zone and try something new. Local theater companies often showcase a wide variety of plays and musicals, from classic dramas to contemporary comedies, providing you with countless opportunities to discover new stories and characters.

In conclusion, think of your retirement years as a beautifully bound book, with each new adventure and experience representing a captivating chapter. As you turn the pages, you'll create a rich tapestry of memories that will fill your heart with joy and fulfillment. Embrace this exciting new phase of your life, for these are truly the best years ahead. By supporting local theater, you're not only enriching your own life but also helping to weave the fabric of your community, making it a more colorful and vibrant place to live.

Bucket List # 86

Visit a Nearby Park or Nature Reserve: Find Tranquility Close to Home

"In Every Walk with Nature, one Receives far more than he Seeks." –John Muir–

Sometimes, all it takes to reinvigorate your spirit is a simple walk in the park. Surrounded by nature's beauty, you can find peace and tranquility right in your own neighborhood. Visiting a nearby park or nature reserve is a wonderful way to immerse yourself in the calming embrace of the natural world, and it's an activity that is easily accessible to everyone, no matter your age or physical ability.

To get started, do a little research on the parks and nature reserves in your local area. You may be surprised to find that there are hidden gems just waiting to be discovered. Make a list of the places you'd like to visit, and consider inviting friends or family members to join you on your adventures. This can be a lovely opportunity to bond with loved ones while enjoying the serenity of nature.

When visiting a park or nature reserve, take the time to truly appreciate the sights, sounds, and smells of the environment. Listen to the birdsong, breathe in the scent of blooming flowers, and marvel at the diverse array of plants and wildlife that call these spaces home.

Take a leisurely stroll, or if you're feeling more adventurous, embark on a more challenging hike to explore the hidden corners of the reserve.

Not only is spending time in nature beneficial for your mental well-being, but it can also improve your physical health. Studies have shown that walking in green spaces can lower stress levels, boost your mood, and even help to alleviate symptoms of anxiety and depression.

In closing, think of visiting a nearby park or nature reserve as a journey into a secret garden, where you can leave the noise and chaos of daily life behind and reconnect with the peace and tranquility of the natural world. Embrace these moments of stillness and let them nourish your soul, for these are the golden years of your life, and they are yours to cherish.

Bucket List # 87

Participate in a Local Sports Event: Embrace Team Spirit and Friendly Competition

"Age is no Barrier. It's a Limitation you put on your Mind." – Jackie Joyner-Kersee –

Participating in a local sports event can be a wonderful way to stay active, make new friends, and embrace the spirit of friendly competition during your golden years. Whether you're a seasoned athlete or a newcomer to the world of sports, there's no better time to dive into this exciting world than now.

To get started, explore the different sports events available in your area. Look for sports clubs, community centers, or recreational leagues that cater to older adults, offering sports such as pickleball, swimming, golf, or even walking clubs. These events are designed to be inclusive and accommodating for people of all skill levels, so don't be shy about giving something new a try!

Once you've found a sports event or club that interests you, reach out to the organizers to learn more about how you can participate. They will be happy to help you find the right fit for your interests and abilities. Remember, the focus of these events is on having fun, staying active, and building connections with others, so don't worry if you're not an expert – the most important thing is to enjoy yourself.

As you begin participating in local sports events, you'll likely find that your physical and mental well-being improves, as well as your social life. Playing sports can help you maintain a healthy weight, reduce stress, and improve your overall mood, while also providing you with opportunities to forge new friendships and share your love of sports with like-minded individuals.

To close with an analogy, think of participating in local sports events as a dance. It's a beautiful way to connect with others, express your-self, and stay active. Each step you take, whether it's trying a new sport or simply cheering on your teammates, adds another layer of joy and excitement to the dance of life.

Bucket List # 88

Discover Your Town's Best Kept Secrets: Go Off the Beaten Path

"Adventure is Worthwhile in Itself." – Amelia Earhart –

Embarking on a journey to discover your town's best-kept secrets allows you to go off the beaten path and experience the hidden gems that make your community special. During your golden years, taking the time to explore and uncover these treasures can lead to new friendships, a deeper appreciation for your surroundings, and a renewed sense of adventure.

To get started, do some research on local history, legends, and lesser-known attractions. Visit your local library or historical society to learn about the stories that make your town unique. You may be surprised by the fascinating tales and landmarks that are just waiting to be discovered.

Make a list of the places you want to visit and start planning your adventures. It could be an obscure park, a tucked-away coffee shop, or a historic building with a fascinating past. Be sure to talk to locals, too – they may have personal recommendations for hidden gems that you won't find in any guidebook.

As you set out to explore, remember to stay open-minded and embrace the unexpected. Sometimes the most memorable experiences come from taking a wrong turn or stumbling upon a delightful surprise. Don't be afraid to veer off course and see where your curiosity takes you.

In your quest to uncover your town's best-kept secrets, you'll not only gain a deeper understanding of the place you call home but also create lasting memories to cherish in the years to come. These experiences will enrich your life and remind you that adventure is always just around the corner.

To end with an analogy, continuing your journey of exploration is like cultivating a beautiful garden. Each adventure, new friendship, and hidden gem you uncover is a vibrant flower, adding color and life to your landscape. With care and dedication, your garden will flourish, and you'll find that the adventure of retirement is more delightful and rewarding than you ever imagined.

Category 12: Embracing New Technologies and Hobbies

Bucket List # 89

Learn to Use Social Media: Connect with Friends and Family Online

"Life is What Happens when you're Busy making other Plans." –John Lennon –

In today's fast-paced world, staying connected with friends and family is more important than ever. With the rise of social media, it's never been easier to share your experiences, learn about others' lives, and maintain relationships across the miles. Embracing social media during your golden years can help you stay informed, engaged, and connected to the people you care about most.

To get started, choose a platform that resonates with you. Whether it's Facebook, Instagram, or Twitter, each platform has its unique features and communities. Start by creating an account, customizing your profile, and inviting friends and family to connect with you. Don't be afraid to ask for help or guidance from tech-savvy family members – they'll likely be more than happy to lend a hand.

As you become more familiar with social media, you'll find endless opportunities to share your life and adventures, as well as stay up-to-date with the latest news, trends, and events. You can join groups or follow pages that align with your interests, allowing you to connect with like-minded individuals who share your passions.

In addition to its social benefits, using social media can help keep your mind sharp and your digital skills up-to-date. By embracing new technologies, you'll not only enhance your online communication but also gain a sense of accomplishment and confidence in your abilities.

In conclusion, think of social media as a colorful garden, filled with vibrant flowers that represent your relationships, interests, and experiences. With time, patience, and care, you can cultivate a thriving online presence that enriches your life and brings joy to those around you. So, go ahead and let your retirement bloom with the endless possibilities that social media has to offer. By embracing social media, you can ensure that your golden years are filled with laughter, love, and connection, making your retirement even more enjoyable and rewarding.

Bucket List # 90

Take a Digital Photography Course: Capture Memories and Master the Art of Editing

"Photography is the Beauty of Life Captured." – Tara Chisolm –

Life is a series of moments, each one fleeting and precious. Taking a digital photography course is a fantastic way to capture these memories and master the art of editing, ensuring that your golden years are filled with beautiful images of the people, places, and experiences you cherish.

To begin your journey into the world of digital photography, find a course that suits your interests and skill level. Many local community centers, colleges, and online platforms offer classes for beginners, intermediates, and advanced photographers alike. Look for a course that covers essential topics like camera settings, composition, and lighting.

Once you've enrolled in a course, immerse yourself in the world of photography. Practice taking pictures of various subjects, from landscapes and architecture to portraits of friends and family. Experiment with different camera settings, angles, and lighting to discover your unique photography style.

As you progress through the course, you'll learn the art of editing your photos using software like Adobe Lightroom or Photoshop. With these tools, you can enhance your images, correct imperfections, and bring your artistic vision to life. Editing is an essential skill for any photographer, allowing you to transform your photos into stunning works of art.

Taking a digital photography course is more than just learning a new skill; it's an opportunity to see the world through a new lens, literally and figuratively. Embrace this creative journey and watch as your perspective on life blossoms and expands.

In the end, embarking on a digital photography journey during your golden years is much like embarking on a road trip. There will be twists and turns, moments of awe and inspiration, and times when things don't quite go according to plan. But with each new experience, you'll grow more confident and capable behind the lens, creating a visual diary of your adventures that you can treasure for years to come.

Bucket List # 91

Start a Blog or Podcast: Share Your Wisdom and Interests with the World

"Don't Let Yesterday take up too much of Today." – Will Rogers –

Starting a blog or podcast during your golden years can be a fantastic way to share your wisdom, interests, and experiences with the world. In this era of digital communication, both platforms allow you to connect with others, exchange ideas, and create a sense of community around your passions.

Why is it important? Well, blogging and podcasting can offer a wealth of benefits, including keeping your mind sharp, fostering creativity, and building relationships with like-minded individuals. Plus, it's a wonderful way to leave a legacy and inspire others with your insights and stories.

To get started, all you need is an idea or theme that excites you. It could be a hobby, a cause you care about, or even a reflection on your life experiences. Next, research the technical aspects of setting up a blog or podcast, such as choosing a hosting platform, setting up your website, and learning to record and edit audio. There are numerous resources available online to help guide you through the process.

Success in blogging or podcasting doesn't happen overnight, and it's essential to stay committed and focused on your goals. Celebrate small victories, learn from setbacks, and always keep moving forward. Once you've got the technical details sorted, create a content plan and schedule. Consistency is key when it comes to building an audience, so aim to publish new blog posts or podcast episodes regularly. Remember, quality is just as important as quantity, so take the time to craft engaging and valuable content.

In conclusion, starting a blog or podcast during your golden years can be an incredibly fulfilling and empowering adventure. Like a gardener nurturing a garden, the time and effort you put into your platform will yield beautiful results that can inspire and uplift those who come across it.

Bucket List # 92

Try Virtual Reality: Immerse Yourself in New Worlds and Experiences

"Age is not a Barrier. It's a Limitation you put on your Mind." –Jackie Joyner-Kersee –

Virtual reality is not just for the young; it's a fantastic way for retirees to explore, learn, and have fun, all while staying active and engaged. It's like having a magic portal that transports you to incredible places and thrilling adventures without ever leaving your home.

Getting started with virtual reality is easier than you think. All you need is a VR headset, which is a device you wear on your head, like a pair of goggles. There are many affordable options available on the market, such as the Oculus Quest or the PlayStation VR. Once you have your headset, you can access a wide variety of games, travel experiences, and educational programs specifically designed for virtual reality.

Virtual reality can help you stay connected with friends and family, even if they are far away. Multiplayer games and social platforms like VR Chat allow you to spend time with loved ones in a virtual environment. You can even join virtual clubs and meet new people who share your interests.

The best part about virtual reality is that it caters to all levels of physical ability. You can choose experiences that suit your needs and preferences, whether you want to sit and relax, or get up and move around. It's a fun and exciting way to stay active and keep your mind sharp during your golden years.

Remember, the sky's the limit when it comes to virtual reality, and you are never too old to try something new. Embracing this technology is like opening a treasure chest of endless possibilities, filled with adventures, activities, and discoveries that will make your retirement years the best years of your life.

As the great Ferris Bueller once said, "Life moves pretty fast. If you don't stop and look around once in a while, you could miss it." Virtual reality is your ticket to stop and look around, experiencing the beauty of life from every corner of the world, and beyond. So go ahead, put on that VR headset, and let your golden years be filled with laughter, exploration, and wonder.

Bucket List # 93

Explore the World of Online Gaming: Find Fun and Camaraderie

"You Can't Help Getting Older, but you don't have to Get Old." – George Burns –

Online gaming offers a vast array of games to suit every taste and interest. From classic card games like bridge and poker to strategy games like chess, and even exciting virtual worlds like World of Warcraft or Second Life, there is something for everyone.

To get started with online gaming, all you need is a computer, tablet, or smartphone, and a stable internet connection. Many games are available for free, while others require a small subscription fee. Simply browse the web or app stores to find games that pique your interest and download them to your device.

One of the most significant benefits of online gaming is the social aspect. Many games feature in-game chat or voice chat, allowing you to interact with other players from all around the world. This is a fantastic opportunity to make new friends, share your experiences, and even learn from others.

If you're looking for a more structured social environment, consider joining online gaming clubs or communities. These groups often host regular events, tournaments, and meetups, giving you a chance to connect with like-minded individuals who share your passion for gaming.

Online gaming can also help keep your mind sharp by challenging you with puzzles, strategy games, and fast-paced action. Research has shown that engaging in mentally stimulating activities can improve memory, cognitive function, and overall brain health, making online gaming an excellent choice for retirees seeking to maintain their mental agility.

As you explore into this thrilling world, always remember that age is just a number, and the spirit of adventure and play knows no bounds. Let online gaming be the spark that ignites your zest for life, transforming your golden years into a time of laughter, learning, and unforgettable memories. Like a master gardener cultivating a lush and thriving garden, you have the power to nurture your retirement years into a flourishing, joy-filled oasis by embracing the world of online gaming.

Bucket List # 94

Learn the Basics of Video Editing: Create Your Own Visual Masterpieces

"Creativity is Intelligence Having Fun." – Albert Einstein
–

Learning the basics of video editing is a fantastic way for retirees to unleash their creativity, preserve precious memories, and even share their unique perspective with the world.

Video editing is more accessible than ever before, thanks to user-friendly software and a wealth of online tutorials. With just a few simple tools and a bit of practice, you can transform raw footage into polished, engaging videos that showcase your creative vision.

To get started with video editing, you'll need a computer or tablet, video editing software, and some video clips to work with. Many devices come with free editing software, like Windows Movie Maker for PCs or iMovie for Macs. If you prefer more advanced features, consider investing in software like Adobe Premiere Pro or Final Cut Pro.

Once you have your editing software, it's time to start learning the basics. There are plenty of online resources, including tutorials, courses, and forums, that cater to beginners. Websites like YouTube and Skill share offer step-by-step guides on how to use various editing tools and techniques.

As you become more comfortable with video editing, consider taking on personal projects that spark your interest. You could create a video montage of your travels, compile a family history, or even produce short films to share with friends and family. Embracing video editing is like taking a blank canvas and transforming it into a vibrant, captivating work of art. With each new project, you have the opportunity to explore your passions, share your stories, and make your golden years truly unforgettable.

As the great artist Vincent van Gogh once said, "Great things are done by a series of small things brought together." Let video editing be the brush that brings together the small, precious moments of your life, painting a rich and colorful tapestry of memories that will be cherished for years to come. Your retirement years are the perfect time to create, discover, and celebrate the beauty that lies within your own unique vision.

Bucket List # 95

Discover New Hobbies through Online Tutorials: Broaden Your Skillset

"Every Accomplishment Starts with the Decision to Try."
– John F. Kennedy –

Retirement is the perfect time to explore new hobbies, learn new skills, and reignite your passion for life. With the vast resources available online, discovering new hobbies and broadening your skillset has never been easier. Online tutorials offer a wealth of knowledge right at your fingertips, enabling you to pursue your interests and find joy in the process of learning and growing.

Online tutorials are an excellent way to explore a wide range of hobbies, from painting and knitting to gardening and woodworking. With countless resources available on platforms like YouTube, Skill share, and Udemy, you can learn at your own pace and master new skills from the comfort of your own home.

To get started, think about the hobbies or interests that excite you. Make a list of activities you've always wanted to try or skills you'd like to develop. Next, search for tutorials or courses online that cater to beginners in your chosen hobby. Many tutorials are available for free or for a small fee, making it easy and affordable to dive into your new pursuits.

As you embark on your journey of discovery, remember to be patient with yourself. Learning a new skill takes time and practice, but the rewards of personal growth and accomplishment are well worth the effort. Embrace the process, and don't be afraid to make mistakes - they are a natural part of learning.

Diving into new hobbies through online tutorials is like opening a treasure chest of knowledge, with each new skill adding a brilliant gem to your collection. With every tutorial, you unlock new opportunities for growth, creativity, and personal fulfillment, making your golden years truly vibrant and rewarding

In the words of author C.S. Lewis, "You are never too old to set another goal or to dream a new dream." Let online tutorials be the key that unlocks the door to a world of endless possibilities, allowing you to embrace new hobbies, ignite your passions, and make your retirement years the most enriching and fulfilling time of your life.

Bucket List # 96

Attend Virtual Events and Workshops: Stay Connected and Keep Learning

"Age is an Issue of Mind over Matter. If you Don't mind, it doesn't Matter." - Mark Twain –

As we embark on our golden years, we must remember that the mind is a powerful tool. One way to keep it sharp and engaged is by attending virtual events and workshops. These digital gatherings provide a fantastic opportunity for us to stay connected with the world, learn new things, and indulge in our passions without leaving the comfort of our homes.

Virtual events and workshops have become increasingly popular, especially since they offer a safe and convenient way to socialize and gain knowledge. Just because we're retired doesn't mean we have to stop learning and growing. Whether you're interested in painting, cooking, or even learning a new language, there's a virtual event or workshop out there waiting for you to join.

To get started, simply search the internet for topics that pique your interest. Many organizations and experts offer free or low-cost virtual events and workshops, so you'll likely find something that fits your budget. Once you've identified a few options, check their websites for registration details and any technical requirements. Most virtual events are hosted on easy-to-use platforms, such as Zoom or Google Meet, making it simple for you to connect and participate.

Don't be shy about diving into this digital world. Attending virtual events and workshops is a wonderful way to meet like-minded individuals, make new friends, and enrich your golden years. You might even discover a new hobby or passion that reignites your zest for life.

Remember, retirement is like a second spring. When the leaves of your career fall away, it's the perfect time for new interests, skills, and friendships to blossom. Embrace this season of life by attending virtual events and workshops, and make your golden years truly unforgettable. The golden years are an opportunity to embrace change and keep moving forward. By attending virtual events and workshops, you'll be able to maintain your balance, stay connected, and keep learning, ensuring that your retirement is filled with laughter, adventure, and personal growth.

Category 13: Reinventing Your Living Space

Bucket List # 97

Declutter and Organize Your Home: Simplify Your Life and Create Space

"Have Nothing in your House that you do not know to be Useful or Believe to be Beautiful."

– William Morris –

Retirement is a time of new beginnings, adventures, and rediscovering the joys of life. One of the best ways to start this exciting journey is by decluttering and organizing your home. Not only will this create a more comfortable and inviting space, but it will also simplify your life and give you the freedom to focus on the things that truly matter.

Decluttering and organizing may sound daunting, but it's much easier than you think. First, take one room or area at a time, so you don't feel overwhelmed. Sort your belongings into three categories: keep, donate, and discard. Keep only the items that serve a purpose or hold sentimental value. Donate the items in good condition that you no longer need or want. Discard the items that are broken, damaged, or have outlived their usefulness.

Next, invest in some simple organizing tools like shelves, bins, or containers. These will help you store your belongings in an orderly and easily accessible manner. Remember, an organized home is a peaceful home. You'll find that by decluttering and organizing, you'll be able to better focus on the adventures and activities that await you in your golden years.

Maintain your organized space by periodically revisiting your belongings and making sure everything is in its proper place. This will help prevent clutter from creeping back in and ensure that your home remains a sanctuary where you can fully enjoy your retirement.

Think of decluttering and organizing like pruning a tree. By removing the dead branches and leaves, you allow room for new growth, better health, and a more beautiful appearance. Your home is no different. By simplifying your space, you create room for new experiences, memories, and a more fulfilling retirement. After all, these are the best years of your life – embrace them with open arms and an open heart.

Bucket List # 98

Redesign a Room: Express Your Personality and Style

"Your Home should tell the Story of who you are, and be a Collection of what you Love."

– Nate Berkus –

Retirement is an opportunity to rediscover yourself and express your unique personality and style. Redesigning a room in your home is a fantastic way to showcase your individuality while creating a space that reflects your passions and interests. This is not only a fun and engaging project but also a chance to transform your living space into a true reflection of your golden years.

To get started, choose a room that you would like to redesign. It could be a bedroom, living room, or even a hobby room – the choice is yours! Begin by envisioning the atmosphere you want to create. Consider colors, textures, and patterns that make you feel happy and inspired.

Determine your budget and prioritize the changes you want to make. You don't have to spend a fortune to create a stunning room. Simple changes like painting the walls, rearranging furniture, or adding new accents can make a significant impact. Don't be afraid to get creative and repurpose existing items in your home.

When selecting new furniture or décor, opt for pieces that reflect your personality and interests. This is your chance to showcase your individuality, so be bold and choose items that make you smile. Remember, this room is a reflection of who you are and what you love.

Redesigning a room is like painting a self-portrait. Each brushstroke represents your unique experiences, passions, and dreams. With every change you make, you're creating a masterpiece that captures the essence of who you are and the life you want to lead during your retirement years. So, go ahead and pick up that paintbrush – it's time to let your creativity shine and create a space that truly reflects your personality and style. After all, these are your best years yet, and your home should be a celebration of that.

Bucket List # 99

Create an Outdoor Oasis: Transform Your Yard into a Personal Paradise

"The Garden Suggests There Might be a place where we can meet Nature Halfway." – Michael Pollan –

Retirement is a time to cultivate new experiences and create spaces that bring joy and relaxation. Transforming your yard into an outdoor oasis is an excellent way to do just that. By creating a personal paradise just steps from your door, you'll have the perfect setting to enjoy your golden years while connecting with nature and making cherished memories with family and friends.

To begin, take a moment to envision your dream outdoor space. Consider how you would like to use the area, whether it's for gardening, entertaining, or simply relaxing with a good book. This vision will guide your design and help you create a space that truly reflects your personality and interests.

Assess your yard's size, shape, and natural features. Work with these elements to create a harmonious and functional design. For instance, if you have a large, sunny area, consider planting a vegetable garden or flower beds. If you have a shaded corner, create a cozy seating area with comfortable chairs and a fire pit.

Incorporate elements that bring you joy and relaxation. This could include water features like a small pond or fountain, outdoor lighting for ambiance, or a pergola draped with climbing plants. Don't forget to add personal touches, such as sculptures, wind chimes, or birdhouses, to make the space uniquely yours.

Creating an outdoor oasis is like composing a symphony. Each element – the plants, water features, and seating areas – represents a different instrument, working in harmony to create a masterpiece that soothes the soul and delights the senses. As you continue to explore and enjoy your personal paradise, remember that these are your best years yet – filled with beauty, adventure, and the chance to connect with the world around you in a truly meaningful way. Remember, these are your best years yet – make them truly magical by creating an outdoor oasis that reflects your unique vision and spirit.

Bucket List # 100

Build a Cozy Reading Nook: Design the Perfect Space for Relaxation

"Adventure is Not Outside man; it is Within." – George Eliot –

A time when you can finally relax and do all the things you've been dreaming of. One of the best ways to enjoy your golden years is by creating a cozy reading nook, where you can indulge in your favorite books and lose yourself in exciting new worlds. This perfect space for relaxation not only offers an opportunity to escape daily stress but also keeps your mind sharp and active.

You may wonder why a reading nook is so important. Well, it's simple. Reading has been proven to have numerous benefits, such as improving mental stimulation, reducing stress, and enhancing knowledge. It's also an enjoyable way to spend time in your retirement years, allowing you to grow and learn at your own pace.

It could be by a window with natural light, in your living room, or even a spare room that you can transform into your reading sanctuary.

- **Choose comfortable seating**: A comfy chair or couch is essential for your reading nook.
- **Add good lighting**: Natural light is perfect for daytime reading, but you'll also need a lamp or two for nighttime reading sessions.
- **Surround yourself with books**: Install shelves or a bookcase to display your favorite books, creating a mini-library just for you.
- **Personalize your space**: Add your favorite decorative items, like cozy blankets, throw pillows, and artwork, to make your reading nook truly your own.

Building a cozy reading nook is like planting a beautiful garden, where you can retreat to a world of vibrant colors, captivating stories, and mesmerizing characters. Each book you read becomes a flower, blossoming with new experiences and wisdom, and your reading nook is the fertile soil that nurtures your mind's growth. Embrace this opportunity to make your golden years truly magical and fulfilling. The world is your oyster, and your reading nook is the pearl hidden within, waiting to be discovered and cherished.

Bucket List # 101

Start a Home Garden: Grow Your Own Herbs, Flowers, or Vegetables

"To Plant a Garden is to Believe in Tomorrow." – Audrey Hepburn –

Embrace the joys of nature and cultivate a new hobby by starting a home garden during your golden years. Gardening is not only a fulfilling and therapeutic activity, but it's also an excellent way to stay active, connect with the earth, and enjoy the fruits (and vegetables) of your labor.

It encourages physical exercise, promotes mental well-being, and provides fresh, homegrown produce that you can take pride in. Moreover, it's a fantastic way to bond with family and friends as you share your gardening journey together.

- **Decide what to grow**: Begin by determining whether you'd like to grow herbs, flowers, vegetables, or a mix of all three.
- **Choose a location**: Find a suitable spot in your yard or on your balcony that receives ample sunlight and has good drainage.

- **Prepare the soil:** Healthy soil is the foundation of a thriving garden. Improve the quality of your soil by adding organic matter, such as compost or aged manure, to provide essential nutrients for your plants.
- **Select your plants**: Purchase seeds, seedlings, or young plants from a local nursery or online store.
- **Plant and nurture**: Water your plants regularly, but avoid overwatering, as this can cause root rot.

Starting a home garden is like creating a living tapestry, where each plant, herb, or flower you grow adds a vibrant thread to the masterpiece. As you nurture your garden, you'll also nurture your soul, discovering new passions and learning valuable lessons about patience, growth, and the beauty of nature.

Cultivating a home garden is like embarking on a thrilling expedition, where each new plant, technique, or gardening experience adds depth and excitement to your journey. Remember, these are your best years ahead, and it's time to celebrate them by embracing the wonder and fulfillment of tending to your very own flourishing garden.

Bucket List # 102

Host a Home Makeover Party: Collaborate with Friends on Fun DIY Projects

"The Best Way to Predict your Future is to Create it." – Peter Drucker –

Unleash your creativity and gather your friends for a fantastic adventure in the form of a home makeover party. This fun-filled event not only breathes new life into your living space but also brings people together for a memorable bonding experience. During your golden years, it's essential to stay engaged, active, and connected with friends and family, and a home makeover party is the perfect opportunity to do just that.

It encourages collaboration, strengthens relationships, and provides a shared sense of accomplishment. Moreover, it's an excellent way to learn new skills and explore your creative potential.

Here are some steps to help you plan and host your very own home makeover party:

- **Choose a project:** Select a DIY project that is manageable, fun, and meaningful to you.

- **Plan the event**: Set a date for your home makeover party and create a list of supplies you'll need for the chosen project.
- **Invite your friends:** Reach out to friends who enjoy DIY projects and would be excited to participate in your home makeover party.
- **Prepare your space**: Clear the area where the project will take place, and have all necessary supplies ready for your guests.
- **Get creative and have fun**: Encourage your friends to contribute their ideas and work together to bring your chosen project to life.

Hosting a home makeover party is like creating a beautiful mosaic with your friends, where each person contributes a unique piece to form a stunning masterpiece. As you collaborate and learn from one another, you'll strengthen bonds and create lasting memories that enrich your golden years.

Remember, your best years lie ahead, and it's time to make the most of them by embracing new experiences and filling your days with laughter, creativity, and companionship. Let your home makeover party be a testament to the power of friendship and the endless possibilities that await you in this incredible chapter of your life.

Bucket List # 103

Learn Feng Shui: Harmonize Your Living Space with Positive Energy

"Your Environment is a Reflection of who you are, and who you are is a Reflection of your Environment." – Marie Diamond –

Embarking on the journey to learn Feng Shui is a delightful and enriching way to harmonize your living space with positive energy during your golden years. Feng Shui is an ancient Chinese practice that focuses on creating balance and harmony in your environment, which in turn, promotes overall well-being and happiness. As you enter this exciting phase of your life, it's essential to surround yourself with positive energy that fosters growth, relaxation, and prosperity.

It encourages mindfulness, enhances your living space, and promotes a sense of peace and tranquility. By integrating Feng Shui principles into your home, you'll create a sanctuary that supports your physical, emotional, and spiritual well-being.

Here's how you can get started:

- **Declutter your space**: A clean and organized environment is the foundation of Feng Shui.
- **Balance the five elements**: Feng Shui emphasizes the importance of balancing the five elements (wood, fire, earth, metal, and water) within your living space
- **Ensure proper lighting**: Natural light is a powerful source of positive energy in Feng Shui.
- **Use color wisely:** Colors play a significant role in Feng Shui, as they can evoke specific emotions and energy.
- **Position furniture strategically**: The placement of furniture in your home can impact the flow of energy.

Learning Feng Shui is like becoming a conductor of an energy symphony, where every element, color, and object in your living space comes together in perfect harmony to create a vibrant and uplifting atmosphere. As you explore this ancient art, you'll gain valuable insights into the interconnectedness of your environment and your well-being, creating a home that supports and nurtures you during your golden years.

These are your best years ahead, and it's time to make the most of them by cultivating a harmonious and joyful living space that reflects the beauty, love, and abundance that reside within you. Let Feng Shui be the compass that guides you toward a more balanced, peaceful, and fulfilling life.

Bucket List # 104

Create a Memory Wall: Display Your Favorite Photos and Mementos

"Memories are the Key not to the past, but to the Future."
– Corrie ten Boom –

Creating a memory wall is a heartwarming and meaningful way to celebrate the cherished moments, people, and experiences that have shaped your life. During your golden years, it's essential to embrace the joy and beauty of your memories, using them as a source of inspiration and motivation as you embark on new adventures and create lasting bonds. A memory wall serves as a visual reminder of the love, laughter, and accomplishments that have filled your life, bringing a sense of warmth and connection to your living space.

Here are some steps to help you get started:

- **Choose a location**: Select a wall in your home that is visible and has enough space to accommodate your favorite photos and mementos.
- **Gather your memories**: Look through your photo albums, keepsakes, and memorabilia to find the items that

hold special meaning and represent your most treasured memories.

- **Plan your layout:** Before attaching anything to the wall, lay out your photos and mementos on the floor or a large table to visualize how they will fit together.
- **Secure your memories**: Use adhesive strips, picture hangers, or a combination of both to securely attach your memories to the wall.
- **Add personal touches**: Enhance your memory wall with meaningful quotes, decorative elements, or artwork that complements your memories and personal style.

Creating a memory wall is like weaving a beautiful tapestry, where each photo, memento, and keepsake represents a unique thread that comes together to form a rich and vibrant story of your life. As you admire your memory wall, you'll be reminded of the love, laughter, and adventures that have filled your days, fueling your desire to make the most of your golden years.

Remember, your best years lie ahead, and it's time to embrace the joy, love, and abundance that await you in this extraordinary chapter of your life. Let your memory wall be a testament to the power of memories and their ability to inspire, uplift, and guide you as you explore the limitless possibilities that lie before you.

Category 14: Embracing Change and Personal Growth

Bucket List # 105

Set Meaningful Goals: Plan Your Future and Stay Motivated

"What you Get by Achieving your Goals is not as Important as what you become by Achieving your Goals."
– Zig Ziglar –

Setting meaningful goals during your golden years is an essential and empowering way to plan your future, stay motivated, and make the most of this exciting chapter in your life. Goals provide direction, purpose, and a sense of accomplishment, helping you maintain an active and engaged lifestyle as you embrace new adventures and experiences.

Here are some tips to help you get started:

- **Reflect on your values**: Consider what is truly important to you, and let your values guide the goals you set.
- **Be specific:** Clearly define your goals and outline the steps you need to take to achieve them.
- **Set SMART goals**: Ensure your goals are Specific, Measurable, Achievable, Relevant, and Time-bound.

- **Break goals into smaller tasks**: Divide your goals into smaller, more manageable tasks, making it easier to stay motivated and see progress.
- **Write your goals down**: Putting your goals on paper makes them more tangible and increases your commitment to achieving them.
- **Share your goals:** Tell your friends and family about your goals to gain their support and encouragement, helping you stay accountable and motivated.

Setting meaningful goals is like embarking on a thrilling voyage across uncharted waters, where each goal serves as a guiding star, leading you towards new discoveries, adventures, and growth. As you navigate the vast ocean of possibilities that await you during your golden years, your goals will provide direction, purpose, and a sense of accomplishment, ensuring that your journey is fulfilling, meaningful, and rewarding.

Remember, these are your best years, and it's time to make the most of them by pursuing your passions, interests, and dreams. Let your goals be the compass that guides you towards a future filled with purpose, joy, and personal growth, as you chart a course towards an exciting, fulfilling, and extraordinary life during your golden years.

Bucket List # 106

Practice Gratitude: Cultivate an Attitude of Appreciation

"Gratitude Makes sense of our Past, Brings Peace for Today, and Creates a Vision for Tomorrow." – Melody Beattie –

As you embark on this exciting journey into your golden years, it's essential to take a moment to embrace the attitude of gratitude. Cultivating an attitude of appreciation not only enhances our well-being but also brings joy and fulfillment to our lives. This magical ingredient can turn the mundane into the extraordinary and give you a fresh perspective on life.

The importance of practicing gratitude cannot be overstated. It helps us to focus on the positive aspects of our lives, keeping our spirits high and allowing us to see the silver lining in every situation. Gratitude also strengthens relationships, as expressing appreciation for the people around us fosters deeper connections and mutual respect.

Getting started with practicing gratitude is simpler than you may think.

Here are a few easy tips to help you embrace this wonderful habit:

- **Keep a gratitude journal**: Dedicate a few minutes each day to jot down the things you're grateful for. It doesn't have to be lengthy; a simple list will do.
- **Express your appreciation:** Don't hesitate to share your gratitude with others. Tell your loved ones how much they mean to you or thank a stranger for their kindness.
- **Make it a ritual:** Find a time each day to reflect on what you're grateful for, whether it's during your morning coffee or before bedtime.
- **Seek the good**: Focus on the positives in every situation, even when things don't go as planned.

Remember, your golden years are a time to cherish and enjoy. By embracing an attitude of gratitude, you will unlock the secret to a fulfilling and vibrant retirement, proving that these truly are the best years of your life.

Cultivating an attitude of gratitude is like planting a garden – the more love and attention you give it, the more it blossoms and bear's fruit. In the same way, the more gratitude you cultivate, the more blessings you'll find in your life. Let it guide you through your golden years, reminding you that the best is yet to come. After all, your retirement is like a beautiful sunrise, and with an attitude of appreciation, you'll witness the most vibrant colors of your life.

Bucket List # 107

Seek Out New Experiences: Step Outside Your Comfort Zone

"Life Begins at the End of your Comfort Zone." – Neale Donald Walsch –

Seeking out new experiences is essential to living a full and exciting life, especially during retirement. It's never too late to step outside your comfort zone and embrace the unknown. In fact, these golden years present the perfect opportunity to explore, learn, and grow.

The importance of trying new things cannot be overstated. When we challenge ourselves, we not only build resilience, but also gain a newfound appreciation for life. Stepping outside our comfort zone can help us stay mentally sharp, develop new skills, and create lasting memories. Moreover, these experiences often lead to increased self-confidence, happiness, and overall well-being.

Getting started might seem daunting, but it doesn't have to be. Begin by identifying areas of interest that you haven't had the chance to explore. Maybe you've always wanted to learn a new language or take up a hobby like painting or dancing. No matter how big or small, choose something that excites you and sparks your curiosity.

Once you have a goal in mind, commit to taking the first step. This might mean signing up for a class, joining a local group, or even just setting aside time to practice your new hobby. Remember, it's okay to feel nervous or uncertain; that's all part of the process. As you begin to embrace these new experiences, you'll find yourself growing more comfortable and confident in your abilities.

Think of life as a vast ocean, and stepping outside your comfort zone is like diving into unexplored waters. It might be scary at first, but as you dive deeper, you'll discover a whole new world filled with beauty and wonder. So, put on your metaphorical scuba gear and take the plunge! After all, these are the best years of your life, and there's no better time to make the most of them.

In conclusion, don't let fear hold you back from seeking out new experiences during your golden years. Embrace the unknown, challenge yourself, and find joy in the process. Remember, life is a grand adventure, and it's up to you to make the most of it. Step outside your comfort zone and seize the day, because the best years of your life are waiting for you.

Bucket List # 108

Develop a Growth Mindset: Embrace Learning Adaptability

"Life Begins at the End of your Comfort Zone." – Neale Donald Walsch –

As you embark on this exciting journey called retirement, remember that your golden years are your best years yet. One incredible way to make the most of this time is by developing a growth mindset. Embracing learning adaptability will not only keep your mind sharp but will also introduce you to a world of new experiences, opportunities, and friendships.

A growth mindset means being open to learning new things, taking on challenges, and being adaptable in the face of change. This is important, especially during your retirement years, as it helps keep your brain active, improves your overall well-being, and encourages personal growth. Moreover, it adds fun and excitement to your life, making every day a new adventure!

Getting started on developing a growth mindset is simple. Begin by setting achievable goals for yourself in areas you've always wanted to explore, such as learning a new language, picking up a musical instrument, or trying out a new hobby. Embrace the process, and don't worry about being perfect; the joy is in the journey itself.

Stay curious and ask questions, just like a child would. This way, you'll continue to learn and grow. Surround yourself with like-minded individuals who share your zest for life and learning, as they can support and inspire you on this journey. And remember, it's never too late to learn something new or to change your perspective on life.

Think of yourself as a caterpillar transforming into a butterfly during this phase of your life. The caterpillar, despite its limited view of the world, has the potential to become something magnificent. Embrace your growth mindset, and you too can spread your wings and soar into a world filled with endless possibilities, laughter, and memories to cherish.

Remember that retirement years are truly your best years, and by fostering a growth mindset, you'll ensure that every moment is filled with laughter, learning, and boundless adventures. So, pick up that brush and paint the vibrant picture of your future, filled with endless possibilities and cherished memories.

Bucket List # 109

Develop a Growth Mindset: Embrace Learning and Adaptability

"Anyone who Stops Learning is old, Whether at Twenty or Eighty. Anyone who keeps Learning Stays Young." – Henry Ford –

Developing a growth mindset is crucial during your golden years, as it allows you to embrace learning and adaptability. By cultivating a mindset that welcomes change and seeks out new knowledge, you'll remain mentally agile and better equipped to face the challenges that life throws your way.

The importance of a growth mindset lies in its ability to foster resilience and a sense of curiosity. When you view challenges as opportunities to learn, you'll be more open to new experiences and more likely to persevere in the face of obstacles. This mindset can lead to increased confidence, happiness, and overall well-being during your retirement years.

To get started, begin by setting small, achievable goals for yourself. These goals can be related to any area of your life, such as learning a new skill, forming healthier habits, or engaging with your community. Break down these goals into manageable steps and celebrate your progress along the way. Remember, the journey is just as important as the destination.

Another way to develop a growth mindset is to adopt a positive attitude towards failure. Instead of viewing setbacks as permanent, see them as valuable learning experiences. Reflect on what you can learn from these situations, and use that knowledge to propel yourself forward.

Think of your life as a beautiful, ever-changing landscape. As you embrace a growth mindset, you'll be like a skilled artist, adding new colors and textures to the canvas with each new experience and lesson learned. The end result will be a rich, diverse, and dynamic masterpiece that reflects the beauty of your golden years.

In conclusion, fostering a growth mindset during your retirement is key to unlocking your full potential and embracing the opportunities that life has to offer. By remaining open to learning and adaptable to change, you'll be better equipped to face challenges and make the most of your golden years. Remember, the best years of your life are ahead of you, so seize the day and paint your own unique masterpiece.

Bucket List # 110

Cultivate Mindfulness: Stay Present and Find Joy in the Moment

"Do not Dwell in the Past, do not Dream of the Future, concentrate the Mind on the Present Moment." – Buddha –

Cultivating mindfulness is a powerful way to stay present and find joy in the moment, especially during your golden years. By practicing mindfulness, you can develop a deeper connection with yourself and the world around you, leading to a more fulfilling and contented life.

The importance of mindfulness lies in its ability to promote mental and emotional well-being. By focusing on the present moment, you can reduce stress, increase self-awareness, and improve your overall quality of life. Additionally, mindfulness can enhance your relationships and help you appreciate the simple pleasures that each day brings.

Getting started with mindfulness is easier than you might think. One of the most effective ways to cultivate mindfulness is through meditation. Set aside a few minutes each day to sit in a quiet, comfortable space, and focus on your breath. As thoughts or distractions arise, gently bring your attention back to your breath without judgment.

Another way to practice mindfulness is by engaging in activities that require your full attention, such as gardening, painting, or even going for a walk. By fully immersing yourself in these experiences, you can learn to appreciate the present moment and find joy in the process.

Think of cultivating mindfulness as tending to a beautiful garden. As you water the plants and remove weeds, your garden will flourish and grow, just as your ability to be present and find joy in the moment will grow stronger with practice. Over time, your garden will become a sanctuary where you can escape the chaos of the world and find peace in the present moment.

In conclusion, practicing mindfulness during your retirement is essential for living a happier and more fulfilling life. By staying present and finding joy in the moment, you'll be better equipped to navigate the challenges and opportunities that life has to offer. Remember, the best years of your life are ahead of you, so embrace the present and let your inner garden flourish.

Bucket List # 111

Nurture Your Relationships: Deepen Connections with Loved Ones

"Connection is the Energy that is Created Between People when they Feel seen, heard, and Valued." – Brené Brown –

Nurturing your relationships is an essential aspect of living a fulfilling life during your golden years. By deepening connections with loved ones, you can create a strong support network that brings joy, companionship, and lasting memories.

The importance of strong relationships lies in their ability to provide emotional support, encourage personal growth, and enhance overall well-being. As you enter retirement, it's the perfect time to invest in the relationships that truly matter.

To get started, make an effort to maintain regular contact with the important people in your life. This might involve calling or messaging friends and family members, organizing get-togethers, or even just writing letters to stay in touch. Don't let distance or busy schedules keep you from nurturing your connections.

Another way to deepen your relationships is by practicing empathy and active listening. When engaging with others, try to put yourself in their shoes and truly understand their feelings and perspectives. This can create a strong bond of trust and understanding between you and your loved ones.

Don't forget to express gratitude and appreciation for the people in your life. Let them know how much they mean to you, and make an effort to celebrate their achievements and milestones.

Think of nurturing your relationships as tending to a precious garden. Each person is a unique and beautiful flower that requires care and attention to bloom to their full potential. With love, understanding, and support, your garden of relationships will flourish, filling your golden years with vibrant colors and sweet fragrances.

In conclusion, investing time and energy into nurturing your relationships during retirement is crucial for leading a rich, fulfilling life. By deepening connections with loved ones, you'll create a support network that brings happiness, growth, and cherished memories. Remember, the best years of your life are ahead of you, so cultivate your garden of relationships and watch it blossom with love and joy.

Bucket List # 112

Discover Your Life's Purpose: Reflect on Your Legacy and Values

"Age is an Issue of Mind over Matter. If you don't mind, it doesn't Matter." – Mark Twain –

Welcome to the wonderful world of retirement. Now that you have the time and freedom to explore life anew, it's the perfect opportunity to discover your life's purpose. Reflecting on your legacy and values is an important step in this journey, as it helps you identify what truly matters to you.

Finding your life's purpose can bring a renewed sense of meaning and happiness to your golden years. It enables you to make meaningful contributions to the world, create lasting memories, and leave a positive impact on the lives of those around you.

Begin by reflecting on your past experiences, passions, and values. Think about the moments that brought you joy, the people who inspired you, and the causes that stirred your heart. Write down your thoughts, and as you do so, you'll start to see patterns emerge.

Consider how you can use your unique skills, talents, and interests to make a difference in the world. Whether it's volunteering, mentoring, or pursuing a new hobby, there are countless ways for you to create a legacy that aligns with your values.

Remember to set realistic goals and break them down into manageable steps. This will make it easier for you to stay committed and make progress. It's also important to be patient and give yourself time to adjust and grow into your new role.

Finally, surround yourself with like-minded individuals who share your passion and can offer encouragement, support, and guidance. This will help you stay motivated and inspired as you embark on this exciting new chapter of your life.

Think of discovering your life's purpose like planting a tree. The seeds you sow today will grow into a beautiful, strong, and vibrant tree that provides shade, comfort, and support for future generations. With every positive step you take, you're creating a lasting legacy that will continue to inspire long after you've gone.

Embrace this incredible journey and remember, your best years are just beginning. The world is waiting for you, and there's no better time than now to start planting the seeds of your legacy. As you continue to explore and embrace this stage of life, you're weaving together a vibrant and cozy quilt that will keep you warm and inspired for years to come.

Category 15: Building Your Dream Retirement Community

Bucket List # 113

Research Senior Living Options: Find the Perfect Fit for Your Lifestyle

"Life is like a Camera. Just focus on what's Important, Capture the good times, develop from the Negatives, and if Things don't work out, just take Another Shot." – Unknown –

Your retirement years are a time for exploration, growth, and finding the perfect fit for your lifestyle. One significant aspect of this journey is researching senior living options. Finding the right environment can have a significant impact on your overall well-being and happiness, as it allows you to live a fulfilling, comfortable, and engaging life.

To begin your search, take the time to assess your needs, preferences, and budget. Consider factors such as location, accessibility, amenities, and the types of activities and social opportunities you desire. Make a list of your priorities, and use this as a guide when evaluating different living options.

There are numerous senior living options to choose from, such as independent living communities, assisted living facilities, or even age-restricted neighborhoods. Attend open houses, take tours, and speak with current residents to get a better understanding of what each option has to offer.

Don't hesitate to involve your family and friends in the decision-making process. Their insights and support can help you make a well-informed choice that suits your unique needs and preferences. Remember that this is an important decision, so take your time and trust your instincts.

Once you've found the perfect senior living option for your lifestyle, embrace the opportunities it presents. Engage in social activities, explore new hobbies, and develop lasting friendships with your neighbors. By immersing yourself in a supportive and stimulating environment, you'll make the most of your golden years.

Think of researching senior living options like trying on a new pair of shoes. The perfect fit will provide comfort, support, and the confidence to stride boldly into the next exciting chapter of your life. Imagine your retirement years as a canvas waiting to be filled with vibrant colors and intricate patterns. Your daily routine acts as the brushstrokes that bring your masterpiece to life. Each day, you have the power to create a beautiful work of art that reflects your unique experiences, passions, and dreams.

Bucket List # 114

Connect with Local Retirees: Develop a Supportive Network

"Alone We can do so Little; Together we can do so Much."
– Helen Keller –

One of the most rewarding aspects of your golden years is the opportunity to connect with fellow retirees and develop a supportive network. Building strong relationships with like-minded individuals can greatly enhance your overall well-being, happiness, and sense of belonging.

Begin by exploring local clubs, organizations, and senior centers that cater to retirees. These venues often offer a wide range of activities, workshops, and social events where you can meet new people who share your interests and passions.

You never know when you might discover a kindred spirit or forge a lasting friendship. Look for opportunities to engage with others, such as volunteering, attending community events, or joining a local sports league.

Another effective way to connect with local retirees is through social media and online forums. There are many groups and communities dedicated to seniors where you can share experiences, exchange advice, and find like-minded individuals who are also seeking to make new connections.

As you build your network of friends and acquaintances, make an effort to nurture these relationships by staying in touch, offering support, and celebrating each other's accomplishments. Remember that friendships, like any other aspect of life, require time and attention to flourish.

Connecting with local retirees is much like assembling a beautiful jigsaw puzzle. Each person you meet represents a unique piece that fits perfectly within the larger picture of your life. As you continue to connect and form bonds with others, the puzzle gradually comes together, revealing a stunning image that reflects the warmth, camaraderie, and joy that comes from a supportive network.

Imagine your retirement years as a beautiful garden, filled with colorful flowers and lush greenery. Volunteering is like tending to that garden, nurturing its growth and helping it flourish. The more you give back, the more vibrant and beautiful your garden becomes, bringing joy and fulfillment to both you and those around you. Start connecting, and remember that your best years are ahead, waiting to be shared with the incredible people you'll meet along the way.

Bucket List # 115

Organize Social Activities and Events: Keep Your Community Engaged and Entertained

"Coming Together is a beginning; Keeping together is progress; Working Together is success." – Henry Ford –

One of the most rewarding ways to make the most of your retirement years is to organize social activities and events that keep your community engaged and entertained. By bringing people together, you can create lasting memories, strengthen relationships, and foster a sense of belonging and unity.

To get started, think about the interests and preferences of your fellow retirees. What types of activities would they enjoy? This could include game nights, movie screenings, potluck dinners, or outdoor outings. The possibilities are endless!

Once you've determined the types of events to organize, reach out to your local senior center, community center, or homeowner's association to secure a space for your gatherings. These organizations are often more than happy to accommodate events that promote social engagement and community spirit.

Spread the word about your upcoming event. Use social media, email, or word of mouth to invite your friends, neighbors, and fellow retirees. Encourage them to invite their friends as well, creating a welcoming and inclusive atmosphere.

Organizing social activities and events can be a wonderful way to give back to your community and keep your golden years filled with laughter, joy, and companionship. By playing an active role in your community, you are helping to create a vibrant and supportive atmosphere where everyone can thrive.

Think of your retirement years as a beautiful dance, with each social activity and event acting as a lively and rhythmic step. As you glide across the dance floor of life, you're bringing people together, creating harmony, and enriching the lives of all who join you in this captivating dance. Take the lead in organizing unforgettable events that will make your golden years truly shine. As you continue to nurture this lively marketplace, you're enriching the lives of all who gather there, creating a thriving and joyful atmosphere that makes your golden years truly unforgettable.

Bucket List # 116

Participate in Community Outreach: Make a Difference in Your Neighborhood

"Act as if What you do makes a Difference. It does." – William James –

Retirement provides the perfect opportunity to participate in community outreach and make a positive impact in your neighborhood. By dedicating time and effort to local initiatives, you can contribute to the well-being of your community, while also discovering a renewed sense of purpose and fulfillment in your golden years.

To begin, identify the areas in your community that could benefit from your support. This could include local schools, hospitals, animal shelters, or environmental organizations. Consider your personal passions and interests, and look for opportunities to make a difference that align with those.

Reach out to the organizations or initiatives that you're interested in supporting. Many groups welcome the involvement of retirees, who bring valuable skills, knowledge, and experience to their cause.

Consider involving your fellow retirees in community outreach efforts. Working together towards a common goal can help strengthen the bonds of friendship and create a sense of camaraderie, while also amplifying the positive impact you can make on your community.

Participating in community outreach is like tending to a garden that you share with your neighbors. As you nurture the plants, pull weeds, and watch your efforts bloom, you're not only beautifying your surroundings but also cultivating a sense of unity and pride within your community. In your golden years, you have the unique opportunity to help this garden grow and flourish, creating a lasting legacy that will be enjoyed by generations to come. Remember, the best is yet to come, and your efforts in community outreach will ensure a brighter future for all.

Imagine your retirement years as a vibrant, colorful tapestry, woven with threads of compassion, dedication, and adventure. Each act of community outreach adds a new hue to the tapestry, creating a stunning masterpiece that reflects your commitment to making the world a better place. Embrace the opportunity to create a legacy of love and hope, knowing that the best is yet to come, and the tapestry of your golden years will become a cherished heirloom for generations to enjoy.

Bucket List # 117

Establish a Retirement Mentorship Program: Share Wisdom and Experience

"Tell me and I forget, teach me and I may Remember, involve me and I learn."

– Benjamin Franklin –

Establishing a retirement mentorship program is a powerful way to share your wisdom and experience with others while simultaneously enriching your own life. By mentoring others, you can create meaningful connections and help guide individuals through their own journeys, offering valuable insights and support along the way.

To begin, identify the skills, knowledge, and experiences that you have gained throughout your life. Think about how these can benefit others, particularly those who may be facing challenges or seeking guidance in their own lives.

Reach out to local organizations, schools, or community centers to inquire about existing mentorship programs or opportunities to create one. Many organizations recognize the value of intergenerational connections and will be eager to collaborate with you in establishing a program.

When developing your mentorship program, consider the needs and interests of your potential mentees. Create a curriculum or outline of topics to cover, including practical advice, personal anecdotes, and lessons learned from your own experiences.

Once your program is in place, be prepared to listen, engage, and provide support to your mentees. Remember, mentorship is a two-way street, and you'll likely learn just as much from your mentees as they do from you.

Establishing a retirement mentorship program is like planting a tree that will provide shade and shelter for generations to come. As the tree grows and matures, it will stand as a testament to your wisdom, experience, and dedication to making a positive impact on the lives of others. Embrace this opportunity to nurture the growth of your mentees, knowing that the best is yet to come, and that your legacy will live on in the hearts and minds of those you've touched. Remember, the simple act of sharing your wisdom can create ripples of change that extend far beyond your wildest dreams.

Bucket List # 118

Advocate for Age-Friendly Policies and Initiatives: Create a Welcoming Environment for All

"Alone We can do so Little; Together we Can do so Much."
– Helen Keller –

Social media can also be a powerful tool for spreading your message and engaging others in your cause. Use these platforms to share success stories, highlight local age-friendly initiatives, and connect with like-minded individuals and organizations. As you embark on your golden years, advocating for age-friendly policies and initiatives can help create a welcoming and supportive environment for all, regardless of age. By promoting inclusive policies, you can ensure that your community remains vibrant, accessible, and enjoyable for everyone.

To begin, educate yourself about the key principles of age-friendly communities, such as accessible public spaces, affordable housing options, and inclusive social activities. Familiarize yourself with the resources available from organizations like the World Health Organization, which offers guidelines and tools to help create age-friendly environments.

Connect with other like-minded retirees who share your passion for creating a more inclusive community. Together, you can form a coalition or advocacy group, pooling your collective knowledge, experience, and influence to promote age-friendly policies and initiatives.

Identify specific areas in your community where improvements can be made and develop actionable plans to address these issues. This may include lobbying for better public transportation, organizing accessible community events, or advocating for the inclusion of older adults in local decision-making processes.

Celebrate your successes and share your experiences with others. By showcasing the positive impact of age-friendly policies and initiatives, you can inspire other communities to adopt similar practices and create a more inclusive world for all.

Advocating for age-friendly policies and initiatives is like building a bridge that connects people of all ages, allowing them to come together in harmony and understanding. As you work to strengthen the bonds between generations, you are helping to create a world where everyone can enjoy the best years of their lives, no matter their age. Embrace the opportunity to leave a lasting legacy of inclusion and acceptance, knowing that the best is yet to come, and that your efforts will create a brighter future for all.

Bucket List # 119

Foster Intergenerational Connections: Bridge the Gap Between Generations

"Coming Together is a Beginning, Staying together is Progress, and Working Together is Success." – Henry Ford –

Fostering intergenerational connections is a powerful way to bridge the gap between generations, share knowledge and experiences, and create a strong sense of community. By nurturing these relationships, you can help to break down barriers, promote understanding, and enrich the lives of both young and old.

To get started, consider volunteering at local schools, community centers, or youth programs. These settings offer ample opportunities to interact with younger generations, share your wisdom, and learn from their unique perspectives.

Another option is to participate in intergenerational programs or events, such as mentorship initiatives, shared hobby clubs, or community projects. These activities provide a platform for meaningful connections and mutual learning, allowing you to forge lasting bonds with individuals from different age groups.

Don't be afraid to reach out to family members, neighbors, or friends from various generations as well. Establishing connections with those closest to you can help to strengthen your existing relationships and create a supportive network of people who span multiple generations.

Finally, approach intergenerational connections with an open mind and a willingness to learn. Each generation has something valuable to teach and contribute, so embrace the opportunity to grow and evolve as you build these bridges.

With each new branch, the tree reaches further, connecting with the world around it and providing shelter and sustenance for countless creatures. As you tend to the tree of intergenerational connections, remember that the best is yet to come, and that the legacy you leave will be one of harmony, understanding, and love, enriching the lives of all who find refuge in its embrace

Fostering intergenerational connections is like weaving a vibrant tapestry of shared experiences, knowledge, and understanding. Each thread represents a unique individual, and as they intertwine, they create a beautiful, intricate pattern that tells the story of a diverse, connected community. Embrace the opportunity to create this rich tapestry during your golden years, knowing that the best is yet to come, and that the legacy you leave will be one of unity, empathy, and shared wisdom.

Bucket List # 120

Celebrate the Achievements and Milestones of Your Fellow Retirees: Recognize and Honor Success

"Success is not Final, failure is not fatal: It is the Courage to Continue that Counts."

– Winston Churchill –

Celebrating the achievements and milestones of your fellow retirees is a wonderful way to recognize and honor their success while fostering a sense of camaraderie and support within your community. By acknowledging the accomplishments of others, you can create an environment of positivity and encouragement, inspiring everyone to strive for greatness in their golden years.

To get started, consider organizing regular gatherings or events to celebrate the achievements of your fellow retirees. These can range from informal potlucks to more formal awards ceremonies, depending on the preferences of your community. The key is to create an atmosphere of genuine appreciation and recognition, where everyone feels valued and celebrated for their accomplishments.

Another way to honor the success of your fellow retirees is to share their stories on social media or in community newsletters. By highlighting their achievements, you can inspire others to pursue their own goals and dreams, creating a ripple effect of motivation and positivity throughout your community.

Don't forget to offer your congratulations and support to those who have reached important milestones. A simple card, phone call, or face-to-face conversation can mean the world to someone who has worked hard to achieve their goals.

Remember that celebrating the achievements of others doesn't diminish your own accomplishments. Instead, it serves as a powerful reminder that success comes in many forms, and that we are all capable of reaching new heights in our golden years. It's a reminder that we are all on this journey together, and that by supporting and encouraging one another, we can achieve great things during the best years of our lives.

Celebrating the achievements of your fellow retirees is like lighting a candle in the darkness. Each small flame represents a unique accomplishment, and as they join together, they create a brilliant, warm light that illuminates the path to greatness for all who follow. Embrace the opportunity to celebrate and honor the success of those around you, knowing that the best is yet to come, and that the legacy you leave will be one of support, encouragement, and shared triumph.

Category 16: Travel and Exploration

Bucket List # 121

Plan a Dream Vacation: Create Your Ultimate Adventure

"Travel is the Only thing you Buy that Makes you Richer."
– Anonymous –

Planning a dream vacation is a fantastic way to create your ultimate adventure and truly embrace the excitement and freedom of your golden years. Traveling not only allows you to experience new cultures, sights, and flavors but also provides an opportunity for personal growth, self-discovery, and lasting memories.

To begin planning your dream vacation, start by identifying your travel goals and preferences. Are you seeking relaxation on a pristine beach, or do you crave the thrill of exploring a bustling city? Do you want to immerse yourself in history and culture, or are you drawn to the beauty of nature? Knowing what you want out of your vacation will help you choose the perfect destination.

Consider all aspects of your vacation, including transportation, accommodations, meals, activities, and any extra expenses. Having a clear budget will help you prioritize your choices and make informed decisions about your dream vacation.

Once you have a destination in mind and a budget set, it's time to start researching. Use travel websites, guidebooks, and recommendations from friends and family to learn more about your chosen location. This research will help you create a detailed itinerary that includes must-see attractions, activities, and experiences.

When planning your vacation, don't forget to consider your personal needs and limitations. Be realistic about your physical abilities, and make sure to include plenty of downtime for rest and relaxation. This will ensure that your trip is enjoyable and stress-free.

Remember that a dream vacation is about more than just the destination. It's about the journey, the experiences, and the memories you create along the way. Embrace the spirit of adventure and make the most of every moment, knowing that your golden years are the perfect time to explore the world and create the ultimate adventure.

Planning your dream vacation is like painting a masterpiece on a blank canvas. Each brushstroke represents a new experience, a cherished memory, or a thrilling adventure. As you add color and texture to your canvas, you create a vibrant, living work of art that reflects the beauty, wonder, and excitement of your golden years. Embrace the journey, and never stop seeking new horizons, for the world is yours to explore, and the best years of your life have only just begun.

Bucket List # 122

Set Sail on a Cruise: Explore the World by Sea

"Life is Either a Daring Adventure or Nothing at All." – Helen Keller –

Planning a dream vacation is a fantastic way to create your ultimate adventure and truly embrace the excitement and freedom of your golden years. Traveling not only allows you to experience new cultures, sights, and flavors but also provides an opportunity for personal growth, self-discovery, and lasting memories.

To begin planning your dream vacation, start by identifying your travel goals and preferences. Are you seeking relaxation on a pristine beach, or do you crave the thrill of exploring a bustling city? Do you want to immerse yourself in history and culture, or are you drawn to the beauty of nature? Knowing what you want out of your vacation will help you choose the perfect destination.

Consider all aspects of your vacation, including transportation, accommodations, meals, activities, and any extra expenses. Having a clear budget will help you prioritize your choices and make informed decisions about your dream vacation.

Once you have a destination in mind and a budget set, it's time to start researching. Use travel websites, guidebooks, and recommendations from friends and family to learn more about your chosen location. This research will help you create a detailed itinerary that includes must-see attractions, activities, and experiences.

Remember that a dream vacation is about more than just the destination. It's about the journey, the experiences, and the memories you create along the way. Embrace the spirit of adventure and make the most of every moment, knowing that your golden years are the perfect time to explore the world and create the ultimate adventure.

Planning your dream vacation is like painting a masterpiece on a blank canvas. Each brushstroke represents a new experience, a cherished memory, or a thrilling adventure. As you add color and texture to your canvas, you create a vibrant, living work of art that reflects the beauty, wonder, and excitement of your golden years. Embrace the journey, and never stop seeking new horizons, for the world is yours to explore, and the best years of your life have only just begun.

Bucket List # 123

Join a Group Tour: Discover New Destinations with Like-minded Travelers

"A Journey is best Measured in Friends, rather than Miles." – Tim Cahill –

Joining a group tour is an excellent way for you to explore new destinations while connecting with like-minded travelers. Sharing experiences and creating memories together can make your journey even more enriching and enjoyable. To get started, research reputable tour companies that cater to your interests, whether that's adventure, history, culture, or a blend of all three.

Once you've selected a tour, be prepared to embrace the excitement of discovery. Engage with your fellow travelers, swap stories, and learn from one another. Participate in group activities, such as guided sightseeing, workshops, and local experiences, to gain a deeper understanding of the places you visit.

As you travel, maintain a positive attitude and be open to trying new things. Sample local cuisine, embrace the local culture, and immerse yourself in the sights, sounds, and smells of each destination. Remember, traveling with a group offers a unique opportunity to forge new friendships and create lasting bonds with those who share your passion for adventure.

Be patient and considerate of your fellow travelers, as you may encounter a variety of personalities and travel styles. Keep in mind that a little flexibility can go a long way in ensuring a harmonious and enjoyable group experience.

Embrace the opportunity to write your own story, one filled with adventure, friendship, and discovery. In the grand tapestry of life, your retirement years are like the final, exciting chapters of a captivating novel – so make every page count and let the adventures unfold.

Embarking on a group tour is like creating a beautiful patchwork quilt. Each member of the group brings their unique fabric of experiences, interests, and perspectives, and together, you'll weave a vibrant tapestry of shared memories that will last a lifetime. As you journey through your golden years, remember that these are the moments worth cherishing – so take the leap, join a group tour, and let the adventure begin.

Bucket List # 124

Embark on a Road Trip: Hit the Open Road and Find Hidden Gems

"Life is Either a Daring Adventure or Nothing at all." – Helen Keller –

Embarking on a road trip is a fantastic way to embrace the adventure of your golden years. With the freedom of retirement, you have the time and flexibility to explore hidden gems and create unforgettable memories. As you hit the open road, you'll be inspired by breathtaking landscapes, charming small towns, and the joy of discovery.

Why is a road trip essential for your ultimate retirement bucket list? Simple. It provides a unique opportunity to reconnect with yourself and others while experiencing the world at your own pace. You'll be able to choose where you want to go and how long you want to stay, making every day an exciting surprise. The laughter, stories, and connections you make along the way will fill your heart with joy and remind you that life is full of wonder.

To begin your road trip adventure, start by selecting your destination. Consider choosing a mix of well-known landmarks and lesser-known attractions to keep the journey diverse and engaging. Next, plan a rough itinerary, but be open to changing it based on discoveries and recommendations from locals. Remember to pack for comfort, including essentials such as a first-aid kit, water, snacks, and a camera to capture memories.

As you travel, make sure to engage with the people you meet. Share your stories, listen to theirs, and forge new friendships. Embrace the spontaneity and freedom that comes with being on the road – visit quirky museums, indulge in local cuisine, and attend community events. The experiences you have will create a tapestry of memories that you'll cherish forever.

Embarking on a road trip is like crafting a beautiful quilt. Each unique square represents a new experience or connection, and when sewn together, they create a masterpiece that captures the spirit of your golden years. As you traverse the open road, remember that this is your time to explore, learn, and grow. The best years are ahead of you, and the world awaits with open arms. Remember, the best years are not behind you, but waiting for you just around the bend. The open road beckons, inviting you to create the masterpiece of your life

Bucket List # 125

Attend a Cultural Festival: Immerse Yourself in Rich Traditions

"Culture is the Widening of the Mind and of the Spirit." – Jawaharlal Nehru –

Attending a cultural festival is a delightful way to immerse yourself in the rich traditions and customs that make our world so diverse and vibrant. In your golden years, embracing new experiences is essential to personal growth and fulfillment, and there is no better way to do this than by celebrating the unique heritage of different communities.

Why is it important to attend a cultural festival during your retirement years? By participating in these celebrations, you not only gain a deeper understanding of the world around you, but also foster a sense of connection with others. Festivals often showcase traditional music, dance, arts, and cuisine, providing an authentic and immersive experience that will create lasting memories.

To get started, do some research to find cultural festivals that spark your interest. These can be local events or international extravaganzas, depending on your travel preferences and budget. Check event calendars, travel blogs, and local newspapers for ideas, and plan your trip around the festival dates.

Once you've chosen your festival, dive into the experience wholeheartedly. Wear traditional clothing if it's appropriate, learn a few phrases in the local language, and taste the authentic dishes. Participate in workshops, attend performances, and make an effort to engage with the locals. The more you immerse yourself, the more rewarding your experience will be.

Attending a cultural festival is like opening a beautifully wrapped gift. The vibrant colors, enchanting sounds, and enticing aromas are like the delicate layers of wrapping paper, ribbon, and tissue that reveal a treasure within – a priceless understanding of the rich tapestry of human culture. As you unwrap each layer, you'll discover that the world is full of wonder and that your golden years hold the promise of endless adventure and growth.

Embrace the beauty of diversity, and let the magic of cultural festivals enrich your life. The best years are yet to come, and there's no better way to celebrate them than by immersing yourself in the traditions that make our world so unique. Attending cultural festivals is like planting a garden of colorful flowers from around the world Continue your journey of cultural exploration and let the vibrant traditions of the world fill your heart with joy and inspiration. The best years of your life are waiting to be discovered, one festival at a time.

Bucket List # 126

Pursue a Themed Vacation: Explore Your Passions Through Travel

"Travel is the Only thing you Buy that Makes you Richer."
– Anonymous –

Pursuing a themed vacation is an extraordinary way to explore your passions and interests through travel during your golden years. By focusing on a specific theme, you'll create a more meaningful and fulfilling experience, allowing you to delve deeper into the things that truly ignite your spirit.

Why is a themed vacation important during your retirement? It offers the opportunity to celebrate your unique interests while also broadening your knowledge and understanding of the world. Whether you're passionate about history, art, wildlife, or food, a themed vacation can enrich your life and create unforgettable memories.

To get started, first identify your passions or interests that you'd like to explore through travel. Consider activities or subjects that have always fascinated you, or rediscover hobbies from your past. Next, research destinations that cater to your chosen theme. For example, if you're interested in history, you could visit ancient ruins or iconic landmarks. If your passion is food, consider taking a culinary tour of a region renowned for its cuisine.

Once you've chosen your destination, create an itinerary that includes activities and experiences related to your theme. This might involve guided tours, workshops, or even attending local events. Be open to expanding your knowledge and trying new things – the more you immerse yourself in your passion, the more rewarding your trip will be.

Pursuing a themed vacation is like creating a unique piece of artwork that represents your interests and passions. Each brush-stroke is a new experience, a new discovery, or a new connection that brings your passions to life. As your masterpiece takes shape, you'll find that your golden years are a time of growth, inspiration, and the pursuit of your dreams.

Embark on a journey that celebrates your passions and let the world be your canvas. The best years of your life are waiting to be explored, one themed vacation at a time. Keep on exploring the world through your passions, and let your themed vacations become the vibrant threads that weave the tapestry of your life. The best years of your life are waiting to be discovered, one adventure at a time.

Bucket List # 127

Connect with Locals: Experience the True Heart of a Destination

"People Don't Take Trips, Trips Take People." – John Steinbeck –

Connecting with locals is an incredible way to experience the true heart of a destination during your golden years. By engaging with the people who call a place home, you'll uncover hidden gems, hear fascinating stories, and gain insights that no guidebook can provide.

Why is it important to connect with locals during your retirement travels? It's simple: locals are the heartbeat of any destination. They possess invaluable knowledge, history, and perspectives that can enrich your journey and transform your trip into a truly unforgettable experience.

Here are some tips to help you connect with locals:

- **Visit local markets, cafes, and community centers**: These are great places to strike up conversations with residents and learn about their daily lives, traditions, and culture.

- **Take part in local events and activities:** Attend community gatherings, festivals, or workshops to immerse yourself in the local culture and create opportunities for connection.
- **Learn a few phrases in the local language**: While you may not become fluent, knowing a few basic phrases can go a long way in showing respect and opening doors for communication.
- **Stay in locally-owned accommodations**: By choosing to stay in a family-run guesthouse or a local bed and breakfast, you'll have the chance to interact with your hosts and gain insider tips and recommendations.

Connecting with locals is like piecing together a beautiful puzzle that represents the essence of a destination. Each piece is a conversation, a shared experience, or a new friendship that adds depth and meaning to your journey. As you fit these pieces together, you'll discover that your golden years are a time of exploration, connection, and endless possibilities.

Let the people you meet along the way become the vibrant pieces of your travel puzzle. The best years of your life are waiting to be lived, one connection at a time. Continue to sow the seeds of friendship and let your garden of connections bloom. The best years of your life are waiting to be cherished, one heartfelt connection at a time.

Bucket List # 128

Volunteer Abroad: Make a Positive Impact While Exploring New Places

"We Make a Living by what we Get, but we make a Life by what we Give."

– Winston Churchill –

Volunteering abroad is a fantastic way to make a positive impact while exploring new places during your golden years. By offering your time, skills, and compassion to communities in need, you'll create lasting change and enrich your own life through unforgettable experiences and connections.

Why is volunteering abroad important during your retirement? It provides a unique opportunity to connect with people from different backgrounds, immerse yourself in new cultures, and make a tangible difference in the lives of others. This combination of adventure and altruism will leave you feeling fulfilled, inspired, and forever changed.

To get started, consider the following steps:

- **Identify your interests and skills:** Reflect on the causes that matter to you and the skills you possess that could benefit others. Whether it's teaching, construction,

healthcare, or conservation, your unique talents can make a difference.
- **Research volunteer organizations and opportunities:** Look for reputable organizations that align with your values and interests.
- **Prepare for your trip:** Once you've chosen a program, learn about the culture and customs of your destination.
- **Stay open and flexible:** Embrace the challenges and rewards of your volunteer experience.

Volunteering abroad is like building a bridge that connects your life to the lives of others. Each brick represents a shared experience, a helping hand, or a moment of understanding that strengthens the bond between you and those you serve. As you build this bridge, you'll discover that your golden years are a time of growth, compassion, and boundless adventure. Each seed represents an act of kindness, a shared smile, or a moment of connection that blossoms into a lasting legacy of positive change.

Set forth on your volunteer journey and let the bridges you build become the foundation of a life well-lived. The best years of your life are waiting to be embraced, one act of kindness at a time. Continue to sow the seeds of kindness and watch as your garden of positive impact flourishes. The best years of your life are waiting to be celebrated, one volunteer experience at a time.

Category 17: Celebrating Milestones and Creating Memories

Bucket List # 129

Throw a Retirement Party: Mark Your New Beginning with a Bang

"Retirement is Not the End of the Road. It is the Beginning of the Open Highway."

Throwing a retirement party is a wonderful way to mark the start of your new beginning with a bang. It's a chance to celebrate your accomplishments, surround yourself with loved ones, and set the stage for the hilarious and unexpected adventures that await you in your golden years.

This milestone event allows you to reflect on the journey that has led you to this moment, while also embracing the excitement and possibilities of the future. It's a time to gather with friends and family, share memories, and create new ones that will become cherished stories in the years to come.

To get started planning your retirement party, consider these simple steps:

- **Set a date and venue:** Choose a date and location that works for you and your guests.

- **Create a guest list**: Invite friends, family, and colleagues who have been a part of your life's journey.
- **Plan the festivities**: Incorporate elements that highlight your interests and passions.
- **Share your retirement bucket list**: Take the opportunity to share your plans and goals for the future with your guests.

Throwing a retirement party is like lighting the fuse of a fireworks display. Each burst of laughter, shared memory, and well-wish ignites the sky, creating a vibrant and dazzling spectacle that marks the beginning of your golden years. As the sparks fly and the colors dance, you'll discover that your retirement is not an ending, but the start of a brilliant new journey.

Your retirement party is just the beginning of a series of celebrations that will define your golden years. Each event, milestone, and adventure are like a colorful balloon, soaring high into the sky and adding brightness and joy to the tapestry of your life. Keep on celebrating, exploring, and connecting. Let the balloons of your golden years carry you to new heights, where the best years of your life are waiting to be discovered, one joyful moment at a time.

Bucket List # 130

Plan a Family Reunion: Strengthen Bonds and Create Cherished Memories

"Family is Not an Important Thing. It's Everything." – Michael J. Fox –

Planning a family reunion during your golden years is a delightful way to strengthen bonds and create cherished memories with your loved ones. As you embark on this new chapter in life, it's the perfect opportunity to celebrate your family's unique story and nurture the connections that make it so special.

Why is a family reunion important in your retirement? It brings together generations, allowing you to share wisdom, laughter, and love. Reunions foster a sense of belonging and create lasting memories that will be treasured by all who attend.

To get started planning your family reunion, follow these simple steps:

- **Set a date and location**: Choose a time and place that works for your family members. Consider factors such as travel distance, accessibility, and the availability of accommodations.

- **Create a guest list:** Compile a list of family members to invite, making sure to include relatives from near and far. Reach out to them early, so they have plenty of time to make arrangements.
- **Plan activities**: Organize a variety of activities that cater to different ages and interests. Games, storytelling sessions, and group photos are just a few ideas to get you started.
- **Share family history**: Make your reunion even more special by incorporating elements of your family's history. Create a family tree, display old photographs, or invite older relatives to share their memories and stories.

A family reunion is like a lush, thriving garden, where each member represents a vibrant bloom, rooted in the rich soil of shared history and love. As you nurture this garden and watch it flourish, you'll discover that your golden years are a time of deep connection, boundless joy, and a celebration of the family bonds that unite us all.

Continue to cultivate your family garden, and let the beauty and love of your golden years blossom. The best years of your life are waiting to be celebrated, one family reunion at a time.

Bucket List # 131

Organize a Surprise Party for a Loved One: Share the Joy of Celebration

"Surprise is the Greatest Gift which life Can Grant Us." – Boris Pasternak –

Organizing a surprise party for a loved one during your golden years is a delightful way to share the joy of celebration and make their special day even more memorable. As you embark on your retirement journey, taking the time to plan a heartwarming surprise for someone you care about can bring happiness not only to them but also to yourself.

Why is organizing a surprise party important? It's a heartfelt gesture that shows your loved one how much they mean to you. It brings people together, creates unforgettable memories, and adds an extra layer of excitement to the celebration.

To get started planning a surprise party for your loved one, consider these simple steps:

- **Choose a date and venue**: Pick a time and location that works for both the guest of honor and the attendees.

- **Enlist help**: Reach out to close friends and family members to assist with planning and preparations.
- **Plan the surprise**: Coordinate with guests to ensure everyone arrives before the guest of honor.
- **Personalize the celebration**: Incorporate elements that reflect the guest of honor's interests and passions, like their favorite colors, hobbies, or foods.

Organizing a surprise party is like creating a hidden treasure chest, filled with laughter, love, and memories. As you carefully plan the celebration and watch your loved one's face light up with joy upon discovering the treasure, you'll be reminded that your golden years are a time for sharing happiness and making unforgettable moments.

Plan that surprise party, create a treasure chest of memories, and let the joy of your golden years sparkle like precious gems. The best years of your life are waiting to be celebrated, one surprise at a time. Let the fireworks of your golden years illuminate the night sky, casting a warm glow over the best years of your life. The most unforgettable moments are waiting to be created, one surprise party at a time.

Bucket List # 132

Host a Themed Anniversary Party: Relive the Magic of Your Love Story

"Love is a Canvas Furnished by Nature and Embroidered by Imagination." – Voltaire –

As you enter your golden years, why not celebrate your love story by hosting a themed anniversary party? Reliving the magic of your journey together is an excellent way to honor your bond, share precious memories, and create new ones with family and friends.

Hosting a themed anniversary party is important because it serves as a beautiful reminder of your love, commitment, and the life you've built together. It's a chance to rekindle cherished memories and bring people together to celebrate the love that has endured through the years.

To plan a themed anniversary party, follow these simple steps:

- **Choose a theme**: Select a theme that is significant to your love story, such as the decade you met, a favorite shared vacation spot, or even the theme of your wedding.

- **Send invitations**: Design invitations that reflect your chosen theme and provide all the necessary details, such as the date, time, location, and any attire requirements.
- **Plan the decorations:** Incorporate elements from your theme into the party decorations.
- **Prepare themed food and drinks**: Create a menu that ties into your theme, with dishes and beverages reminiscent of the era or location you've chosen.
- **Share memories**: Invite guests to share their favorite memories or stories about your relationship.

Each page captures a moment in time, filled with laughter, tears, and tender embraces. As you turn the pages together, you'll be reminded that your golden years are an opportunity to continue adding to your beautiful love story, creating new memories that will last a lifetime.

Host that themed anniversary party, relive the magic of your love story, and remember that your best years are still ahead. Let your love continue to grow and flourish, like a garden nurtured by the warm sunshine of your golden years. Continue to paint the canvas of your love story, one themed anniversary party at a time. Let your love be the inspiration and the joy of your golden years be the vibrant colors that bring your masterpiece to life. Your best years are still ahead, waiting to be captured in the beautiful art of love and celebration.

Bucket List # 133

Create a Memory Box: Preserve Your Most Treasured Keepsakes

"Memory is the Diary that we All Carry about with Us." – Oscar Wilde –

As you embark on your golden years, filled with new adventures and experiences, it's essential to preserve the memories that have shaped your life. Creating a memory box is a wonderful way to cherish your most treasured keepsakes and ensure that they remain a lasting part of your personal history.

A memory box is important because it serves as a physical reminder of the people, places, and experiences that have brought joy, love, and meaning to your life. It's a unique collection of mementos that tell the story of your journey and the memories you've made along the way.

To create your memory box, follow these simple steps:

- **Choose a box:** Select a box that is both durable and visually appealing. I

- **Gather your keepsakes**: Collect items that hold special meaning to you, such as photos, letters, souvenirs, or small trinkets.
- **Organize your keepsakes**: Arrange your mementos in a way that tells a story or follows a chronological order.
- **Personalize your memory box**: Decorate the exterior of the box with paint, stickers, or other embellishments that reflect your personality and the contents of the box.
- **Create a ritual:** Set aside time each year to go through your memory box, reminiscing about the memories it holds and adding new keepsakes to the collection.

Embrace this opportunity to create a memory box that captures your most cherished moments and tells the story of your life's adventures. Your best years lie ahead, filled with new experiences, discoveries, and memories, just waiting to be woven into the fabric of your unique and beautiful tapestry.

Create your memory box and preserve the memories that have made your life extraordinary. Remember that your golden years are an opportunity to continue sowing new seeds of joy, laughter, and love, ensuring that your memory garden remains vibrant and ever-growing. Your best years are still ahead, just waiting to be captured and treasured in your memory box.

Bucket List # 134

Craft a Family Cookbook: Pass Down Beloved Recipes and Stories

"Recipes Don't Work Unless You Use your Heart!" – Dylan Jones –

Food has the power to unite us, evoke memories, and tell stories. Crafting a family cookbook is an opportunity to pass down beloved recipes, share treasured memories, and strengthen the bonds between generations. It's a meaningful project that allows you to preserve your family's culinary heritage and celebrate the unique flavors and traditions that have nourished your loved ones through the years.

Creating a family cookbook is important because it captures a snapshot of your family's history, tastes, and stories. It's a legacy that can be handed down through generations, allowing your children, grandchildren, and beyond to connect with their roots and experience the joy of cooking and sharing meals together.

To get started on crafting your family cookbook, follow these simple steps:

- **Gather recipes:** Reach out to family members and ask them to contribute their favorite recipes, along with any special memories or stories associated with the dish.
- **Organize the recipes:** Sort the recipes into categories, such as appetizers, main courses, desserts, or by family members or occasions.
- **Include personal touches**: Add photos, anecdotes, or family stories alongside each recipe to make the cookbook feel more personal and engaging.
- **Design the layout:** Choose a visually appealing format for your cookbook.
- **Print and share:** Once your family cookbook is complete, print copies for family members or share it digitally, allowing everyone to experience the joy of cooking and sharing these treasured recipes.

Embrace this opportunity to sow the seeds of your family's culinary heritage and watch as your garden blooms, nourishing future generations with the love, warmth, and wisdom of your shared experiences. These golden years are the perfect time to embark on this delightful journey, as you harvest the fruits of your life's experiences and plant the seeds for a lasting legacy.

Gather your favorite recipes, share the stories behind them, and weave together a culinary tapestry that will nourish your family for years to come. Remember, your golden years are the perfect time to embark on this delicious adventure, as you have a wealth of experience and memories to share. Your best years are still ahead, filled with the joy of passing down beloved recipes and creating new memories in the kitchen.

Bucket List # 135

Compile a Photo Album or Scrapbook: Chronicle Your Adventures and Experiences

"Life is Like a Camera. Just focus on what's Important, Capture the Good Times, Develop from the Negatives, and if things don't work out, Just take Another Shot." – Unknown –

Creating a photo album or scrapbook is a wonderful way to preserve your life's adventures and experiences. These treasured collections allow you to relive your memories and share your stories with family and friends.

Here are some simple steps to help you get started on this meaningful project:

- **Gather your materials:** Collect your favorite photos, mementos, and keepsakes, such as postcards, ticket stubs, and travel brochures.
- **Organize your memories:** Sort your photos and keepsakes by theme, event, or timeline.

- **Embellish your pages:** Add decorative elements such as stickers, stamps, and colorful paper to give your album or scrapbook a personalized touch.
- **Involve your loved ones:** Invite family members and friends to contribute their own photos, memories, and ideas to your project. T
- **Keep it updated**: As you continue to embark on new adventures and experiences, add to your album or scrapbook to keep it current and fresh.

Creating a photo album or scrapbook is like weaving a beautiful quilt, each square representing a cherished memory or experience. As you continue to stitch together the fabric of your life, you'll create a warm and comforting blanket that can be shared and enjoyed by all who gather beneath it.

Embrace the joy and fulfillment that comes with creating a tangible record of your life's journey. Your golden years are a time to reflect on the past and embrace the present, and there's no better way to do that than by preserving your memories and experiences in a beautiful and meaningful way.

A photo album or scrapbook is like a treasure chest, filled with precious gems and golden memories. As you open the chest and explore its contents, you'll rediscover the laughter, love, and joy that have filled your life. By compiling this collection of memories, you're creating a lasting legacy that can be shared and enjoyed by generations to come.

Your golden years are an opportunity to celebrate and cherish the moments that have shaped your life. Gather your treasures, and let your creativity shine as you create a beautiful testament to the rich tapestry of your life's experiences.

Bucket List # 136

Write Your Memoir: Share Your Journey with Future Generations

"Life Can Only be Understood Backwards; but it must be lived Forwards."

– Søren Kierkegaard –

When you reflect on your life's journey, it's like watching the sunset paint the sky with colors of gold, pink, and purple. Each shade holds a memory, a story, a piece of your heart. The Ultimate Retirement Bucket List encourages you to embrace the wonderful opportunity of writing your memoir, as it's a chance to share your journey with future generations.

Why is writing a memoir important? It's a treasure chest of your life experiences, lessons, and wisdom. Your family and friends will love reading about your adventures, your heartaches, and your victories. By sharing your story, you create a beautiful legacy that will inspire and guide those who come after you.

So, how do you get started? Think of your life as a giant puzzle with many pieces. To create your memoir, begin by jotting down your memories, big or small. Use photographs, letters, and keepsakes as inspiration. Start with your childhood, and work your way up to the present. Don't worry about making it perfect from the beginning – just focus on getting your thoughts on paper.

Organize your memories into chapters, focusing on the moments that shaped you. Write from your heart, and let your emotions flow. Remember, this is your story, and it's unique to you. Once you've written your memoir, consider sharing it with your loved ones. You might even want to join a writing group or attend a memoir-writing workshop for additional support and guidance.

As you embark on this writing journey, think of your memoir like a quilt. Each patch represents a memory, an adventure, a lesson learned. As you sew these patches together, you create a beautiful, colorful quilt that will warm the hearts of those you leave behind.

Embrace the joy of writing your memoir and celebrate the incredible life you've lived. Go ahead and write your memoir with enthusiasm and pride. Let your golden years be filled with the excitement of sharing your journey and leaving a lasting legacy for those who follow in your footsteps. Remember, the best years are still ahead of you, and every word you write brings new adventures and discoveries to life.

Category 18: Pursuing Lifelong Learning and Intellectual Growth

Bucket List # 137

Enroll in a College or University Course: Keep Your Mind Sharp

"Anyone Who Stops learning is old, Whether at Twenty or Eighty. Anyone who keeps Learning Stays Young." – Henry Ford –

Just like a beautiful flower that never stops blooming, your mind has the power to grow and flourish throughout your golden years. The Ultimate Retirement Bucket List encourages you to tap into this potential by enrolling in a college or university course. This is an incredible opportunity to keep your mind sharp, explore new interests, and make new friends who share your passion for learning.

Why is enrolling in a course important? Education is the key that unlocks the door to personal growth and lifelong fulfillment. Learning stimulates your brain, fosters creativity, and broadens your horizons. By diving into a new subject, you'll not only expand your knowledge but also give your brain a healthy workout.

So, how do you get started? First, identify a subject that piques your interest. It could be anything from art history to astronomy, or from creative writing to computer programming. Then, search for local colleges or universities that offer courses in your chosen field. Many institutions even provide special discounts or free classes for seniors, making it easy to continue your education without breaking the bank.

Once you've found a course that suits your interests, go ahead and enroll! Embrace this new adventure with an open mind and a thirst for knowledge. Remember, there's no age limit to learning, and you're never too old to pursue your dreams.

As you embark on this exciting chapter in your life, think of your brain as a garden. With every new course, you plant the seeds of knowledge, curiosity, and wisdom. As you nurture these seeds with dedication and passion, they'll grow into a magnificent garden, filled with the colorful blossoms of your newfound talents and expertise.

Take a step towards a brighter, more fulfilling future by enrolling in a college or university course today. Remember, the best years are still ahead, and the world of learning is waiting to welcome you with open arms. Embrace this opportunity, and let your mind flourish in the vibrant garden of knowledge.

Bucket List # 138

Join a Book Club: Connect with Fellow Literary Enthusiasts

"There is No Friend as Loyal as a Book." – Ernest Hemingway –

Imagine a world filled with fascinating characters, thrilling adventures, and heartwarming tales. In this magical realm, you can travel to far-off lands, unravel mysteries, and gain insights into the human experience. The Ultimate Retirement Bucket List invites you to explore this enchanting world by joining a book club, where you can connect with fellow literary enthusiasts, share your love for reading, and embark on unforgettable journeys through the pages of great novels.

A book club is a wonderful way to enrich your reading experience by discussing your thoughts, feelings, and perspectives with others. It provides an opportunity to learn from one another, forge lasting friendships, and gain a deeper appreciation for the written word.

Begin by searching for book clubs in your local community. You can find them through libraries, bookstores, or online forums dedicated to your favorite genres. Alternatively, consider starting your own book club by inviting friends, family, or neighbors who share your love for reading.

Once you've joined or formed a book club, embrace the adventure with an open mind and a curious spirit. Read each book with enthusiasm, and don't be afraid to share your opinions, ask questions, or offer insights during discussions. Remember, everyone's perspective is unique, and each voice adds depth and richness to the conversation.

As you immerse yourself in the world of book clubs, think of your reading experience as a vibrant tapestry. Each thread represents a character, a plot twist, or an emotion evoked by the stories you read. As you share your thoughts and connect with fellow readers, these threads weave together to form a beautiful, intricate pattern that represents the collective wisdom and joy found in the pages of great literature.

Embark on this literary adventure with excitement and anticipation. Remember, your golden years are a time for exploration, connection, and the discovery of new worlds. By joining a book club, you're opening the door to countless enriching experiences and creating lasting memories that will warm your heart for years to come.

Bucket List # 139

Attend Lectures or Workshops: Stay Curious and Expand Your Horizons

"Curiosity is the Wick in the Candle of Learning." – William Arthur Ward –

Picture a world of endless possibilities, where you can explore new ideas, unlock hidden talents, and ignite your curiosity. The Ultimate Retirement Bucket List invites you to dive into this world by attending lectures or workshops, as they offer a fantastic way to stay curious, expand your horizons, and embark on a lifelong journey of learning and discovery.

Why is attending lectures or workshops important? These events provide a unique opportunity to broaden your knowledge, cultivate new interests, and connect with experts in various fields. By attending lectures or workshops, you can sharpen your mind, ignite your creativity, and foster a sense of personal growth and fulfillment.

Begin by researching local venues such as libraries, community centers, or museums that host lectures or workshops. Look for events that pique your interest, whether it's a lecture on ancient history, a photography workshop, or a cooking demonstration. You can also search online for webinars or virtual workshops that cater to your interests.

Once you've found an event that intrigues you, don't hesitate to sign up and attend. Embrace this new adventure with an open mind and a willingness to learn. Participate actively by asking questions, engaging in discussions, and taking notes to help you retain the valuable information you'll gain.

As you immerse yourself in the world of lectures and workshops, imagine your mind as a kaleidoscope. With each new idea or skill, you acquire, the kaleidoscope shifts, creating dazzling new patterns of color and light. The more you learn, the more vibrant and intricate these patterns become, reflecting the beauty and richness of your ever-expanding horizons.

Take the first step towards a brighter, more fulfilling future by attending lectures or workshops today. Remember, your golden years are a time for exploration, growth, and the pursuit of new passions. With curiosity as your guide and the world as your classroom, there's no limit to the wonders you'll discover and the adventures that await.

Bucket List # 140

Learn a New Language: Unlock the Door to New Cultures and Opportunities

"Learning Another Language is not Only Learning Different Words for the same things, but Learning Another way to Think about Things." – Flora Lewis –

Imagine a world where you can communicate with people from all corners of the globe, forging connections and unlocking the door to new cultures and opportunities. The Ultimate Retirement Bucket List encourages you to embark on this exciting journey by learning a new language, an adventure that will not only challenge your mind but also enrich your soul.

Why is learning a new language important? Mastering a new language allows you to interact with others on a deeper level, bridging cultural gaps and fostering understanding. It also enhances your cognitive abilities, improves memory, and boosts your problem-solving skills. Plus, it opens up a world of opportunities to travel, make new friends, and explore diverse cuisines, traditions, and art forms.

First, choose a language that sparks your interest, whether it's due to personal heritage, travel aspirations, or simply fascination with its sounds and structure. Explore various learning methods such as language apps, online courses, or local language classes tailored to your learning style and goals.

Once you've found the right resources, commit to a regular study routine, and practice your new language as often as possible. Connect with native speakers, join language exchange groups, or attend cultural events to immerse yourself in the language and gain valuable real-life experience.

As you delve into the world of language learning, picture your mind as an ever-growing library. Each new word, phrase, or grammatical rule you learn is like a book added to the shelves, expanding your knowledge and understanding of the world. The more languages you learn, the vaster and more diverse your mental library becomes, reflecting the beauty and richness of human culture.

Take the plunge and learn a new language today. Remember, your golden years are a time for discovery, growth, and the pursuit of new passions. With each word you master, you're unlocking the door to an incredible world of adventure and connection, reminding you that the best years are still ahead.

Bucket List # 141

Take Up a Musical Instrument: Discover the Joy of Creating Music

"Music gives a Soul to the universe, Wings to the Mind, Flight to the Imagination, and Life to Everything." – Plato

–

Envision a world where your fingers dance across the keys of a piano, your breath brings life to a flute, or your hands strum the strings of a guitar, creating beautiful melodies that resonate in the hearts of those who listen. The Ultimate Retirement Bucket List invites you to explore this world by taking up a musical instrument, a delightful adventure that will not only bring joy to your life but also inspire those around you.

Why is learning a musical instrument important? Playing an instrument offers a multitude of benefits, including improved cognitive function, reduced stress, and increased creativity. It also provides a sense of accomplishment, fosters self-expression, and strengthens your connection with others through the universal language of music.

First, choose an instrument that appeals to you, whether it's based on the sound it produces, the way it's played, or the ease of learning.

Next, research local music schools, private teachers, or online lessons to find the right instruction for your needs and goals.

Once you've found the right resources, set aside regular practice time and approach your musical journey with patience and persistence. Embrace the learning process, celebrate your progress, and remember that even the most accomplished musicians were once beginners too.

As you dive into the world of music, imagine your life as a beautiful symphony. Each note you play represents a cherished memory, a dream, or a moment of happiness. As you continue to learn and grow, your symphony becomes more intricate and harmonious, a testament to your dedication and passion for creating music.

Take up a musical instrument today and discover the joy that comes from making music. Remember, your golden years are a time for exploration, creativity, and the pursuit of new passions. Embrace this opportunity to create your own unique symphony, and let the music you make be a reminder that the best years are still ahead.

Bucket List # 142

Explore the World of Astronomy: Unravel the Mysteries of the Cosmos

"The Nitrogen in our DNA, the Calcium in our Teeth, the iron in our Blood, the Carbon in our Apple pies were made in the Interiors of Collapsing Stars. We are made of Star stuff."

– Carl Sagan –

Imagine a world filled with twinkling stars, mesmerizing galaxies, and awe-inspiring celestial events, a world where you can uncover the mysteries of the cosmos and explore the vast expanse of the universe. The Ultimate Retirement Bucket List beckons you to embark on this exciting journey by delving into the world of astronomy, an adventure that will not only ignite your curiosity but also deepen your appreciation for the wonders of our universe.

Why is exploring astronomy important? Astronomy offers a unique opportunity to connect with the natural world, expand your understanding of the cosmos, and marvel at the vastness and beauty of the universe. It also fosters critical thinking, problem-solving skills, and a sense of wonder that transcends the boundaries of our planet.

How do you get started? Begin by familiarizing yourself with the night sky. Learn about the constellations, the phases of the moon, and the visible planets. Invest in a pair of binoculars or a telescope to enhance your stargazing experience, and consider joining a local astronomy club or attending stargazing events to connect with fellow enthusiasts.

Once you've dipped your toes into the world of astronomy, dive deeper by reading books, watching documentaries, or enrolling in online courses. Embrace the adventure with an open mind, and let your curiosity guide you as you explore the celestial wonders that await.

As you venture into the realm of astronomy, think of the night sky as an infinite canvas painted with the stories of countless celestial objects. Each star, planet, and galaxy has a tale to tell, and as you unravel these mysteries, you add your own brushstrokes to the ever-evolving masterpiece that is our universe.

Set your sights on the cosmos and begin your astronomical journey today. Remember, your golden years are a time for exploration, growth, and the pursuit of new passions. By exploring the world of astronomy, you're opening the door to a universe of wonder, reminding you that the best years are still ahead.

Bucket List # 143

Join a Trivia Team: Test Your Knowledge and Make New Friends

"The More you Know, the More you Realize you know Nothing." – Socrates –

Picture a world where you can challenge your mind, share your wealth of knowledge, and forge new friendships, all while having a blast. The Ultimate Retirement Bucket List encourages you to dive into this world by joining a trivia team, an exhilarating adventure that will not only keep your brain sharp but also help you connect with others who share your love for learning.

Why is joining a trivia team important? Participating in trivia events allows you to test your knowledge, learn new facts, and engage in friendly competition. It also promotes social interaction, teamwork, and a sense of camaraderie, which can have a positive impact on your overall well-being and happiness.

How do you get started? Begin by researching local trivia nights at pubs, restaurants, or community centers. Look for events that cater to a wide range of topics or themes that pique your interest. Alternatively, you can search online for virtual trivia events or apps that allow you to participate from the comfort of your own home.

Once you've found a trivia event that intrigues you, gather a group of friends or family members to form a team, or simply show up and join an existing team. Embrace the challenge with enthusiasm and a willingness to learn, and don't forget to celebrate your team's victories, no matter how small.

As you immerse yourself in the world of trivia, imagine your brain as a treasure chest filled with precious gems, each representing a unique piece of knowledge you've acquired throughout your life. By joining a trivia team, you're not only adding new gems to your collection but also sharing your wealth of knowledge with others, creating a dazzling display of brilliance and camaraderie.

Take the leap and join a trivia team today. Remember, your golden years are a time for exploration, growth, and the pursuit of new passions. By testing your knowledge and making new friends, you're embracing the fun and adventure that await, reminding you that the best years are still ahead.

Bucket List # 144

Pursue a Continuing Education Certificate: Master a New Skill or Subject

"Education is the Passport to the Future, for Tomorrow Belongs to those who prepare for it today." – Malcolm X –

Imagine a world where you can expand your horizons, master new skills, and explore subjects that spark your curiosity. The Ultimate Retirement Bucket List invites you to experience this world by pursuing a continuing education certificate, an enlightening adventure that will not only enhance your knowledge but also enrich your life in countless ways.

Why is pursuing a continuing education certificate important? By furthering your education, you're investing in your personal growth, boosting your confidence, and staying mentally sharp. Continuing education also opens doors to new opportunities, whether it's enhancing your career or pursuing a newfound passion.

Begin by identifying a subject or skill that interests you, whether it's related to your profession, a hobby, or a topic you've always wanted to explore. Research local colleges, universities, or online platforms that offer continuing education programs, and choose a course that aligns with your goals and aspirations.

As you delve deeper into your chosen subject, don't be afraid to ask questions, share your insights, and collaborate with your classmates. These interactions will not only help you solidify your understanding of the material but also enable you to forge meaningful connections with like-minded individuals.

Once you've enrolled in a program, commit to your studies by setting aside regular study time and engaging in the learning process. Embrace the challenges and celebrate your accomplishments, knowing that you're expanding your knowledge and creating a more fulfilling life.

As you embark on your continuing education journey, imagine your mind as a garden filled with vibrant, blooming flowers. Each new skill or subject you learn adds another colorful blossom to your garden, creating a rich tapestry of knowledge that flourishes with each passing day.

Take the first step towards pursuing a continuing education certificate today. Remember, your golden years are a time for exploration, growth, and the pursuit of new passions. By mastering a new skill or subject, you're nurturing your personal garden of knowledge, reminding you that the best years are still ahead.

Category 19: Connecting with Nature and the Great Outdoors

Bucket List # 145

Try Birdwatching: Observe the Beauty and Diversity of Avian Life

"In Order to See birds, it is Necessary to become a Part of the Silence." – Robert Lynd –

Imagine a world where you can connect with nature, observe the beauty of the skies, and uncover the secrets of our feathered friends. The Ultimate Retirement Bucket List encourages you to experience this world by trying birdwatching, an awe-inspiring adventure that will not only bring you closer to the wonders of the natural world but also offer you a serene and captivating hobby.

Why is birdwatching important? By observing birds, you're developing a deeper appreciation for the beauty and diversity of avian life. Birdwatching also promotes relaxation, mindfulness, and a sense of connection with nature, which can enhance your overall well-being and happiness.

So, how do you get started? Begin by researching common bird species in your area, familiarizing yourself with their appearances and behaviors. Invest in a good pair of binoculars and a field guide to help you identify and learn about the birds you encounter. Choose a suitable location, such as a park, nature reserve, or even your own backyard, and set out early in the morning or late in the afternoon when birds are most active.

As you embark on your birdwatching journey, take the time to observe and appreciate the intricate details of each bird's appearance, song, and behavior. Stay quiet, patient, and open-minded, allowing yourself to be fully immersed in the experience.

As you delve into the world of birdwatching, imagine your mind as a vast sky filled with the vibrant colors and melodies of various bird species. Each new bird you discover adds another brushstroke to the canvas, painting a rich tapestry of life that celebrates the beauty and diversity of our natural world.

Take the first step towards exploring the captivating world of birdwatching today. Remember, your golden years are a time for discovery, serenity, and the pursuit of new passions. By observing the beauty and diversity of avian life, you're reminding yourself that the best years are still ahead, and the sky is truly the limit.

Bucket List # 146

Take Up Gardening: Cultivate a Green Thumb and Create an Oasis

"To Plant a Garden is to Believe in Tomorrow." – Audrey Hepburn –

Welcome to the enchanting world of gardening, a fulfilling and life-affirming hobby that will transform your golden years into a vibrant and flourishing oasis. The Ultimate Retirement Bucket List invites you to cultivate a green thumb and immerse yourself in the wonders of nature, right in the comfort of your own home.

Why is gardening important? Gardening allows you to connect with nature, practice mindfulness, and enjoy the satisfaction of nurturing life. As you watch your plants grow and thrive, you're also nurturing your own well-being, both mentally and physically.

How can you get started? Begin by researching plants that are suitable for your climate and the space you have available. Consider your personal preferences, such as flowers, vegetables, or herbs, and choose plants that appeal to your senses and interests. Gather the necessary tools, such as gloves, a trowel, and a watering can, and prepare the soil for planting.

Once you've planted your garden, remember to water, weed, and care for your plants regularly. Observe their growth, take note of changes, and celebrate the small victories as your garden comes to life. As you tend to your plants, allow yourself to be fully present, enjoying the sights, smells, and sounds of your blossoming oasis.

Think of your gardening journey as a symphony, with each plant representing a different instrument. As you nurture your garden, the instruments come together, creating a harmonious and beautiful masterpiece that reflects your love and dedication. Your garden is a living testament to the power of patience, resilience, and growth.

Embrace the joys of gardening and let it enrich your golden years with a sense of purpose, wonder, and fulfillment. Just like the blooming flowers in your garden, your retirement years are a testament to the boundless beauty and potential that await you. Remember, the best is yet to come, and with each new bud and blossom, you're painting a breathtaking masterpiece of hope, growth, and renewal.

Bucket List # 147

Go Camping or Glamping: Reconnect with Nature and Find Inner Peace

"In Every Walk with Nature, one Receives far more than he Seeks." –John Muir –

The Ultimate Retirement Bucket List invites you to embark on a thrilling adventure into the great outdoors with camping or glamping. Whether you prefer the rustic simplicity of camping or the luxurious comforts of glamping, reconnecting with nature is a powerful way to find inner peace and embrace the beauty of the world around you during your golden years.

Why is it important to go camping or glamping? Spending time in nature has numerous physical, mental, and emotional benefits. It reduces stress, improves mood, and provides a sense of accomplishment as you learn to navigate and appreciate the natural world. Camping and glamping also offer opportunities for bonding with loved ones and creating lasting memories.

How can you get started? First, decide whether you prefer camping or glamping. Camping involves setting up a tent and sleeping under the stars, while glamping offers a more luxurious experience with amenities like comfortable beds, electricity, and even private bathrooms.

Research campgrounds or glamping sites that cater to your interests and comfort level. Consider factors such as location, facilities, and activities available on-site. Once you've chosen your destination, make a reservation and start preparing for your adventure.

Gather essential gear, such as a tent, sleeping bags, and cooking equipment for camping, or ensure your glamping accommodation provides the necessary amenities. Don't forget to pack appropriate clothing, food, and any personal items you may need.

Think of your camping or glamping adventure as an opportunity to unplug from the hustle and bustle of everyday life, like a painter stepping back from their canvas to gain perspective. As you immerse yourself in the tranquility of nature, you'll discover a newfound appreciation for the beauty and wonder of the world around you.

Camping and glamping are much like the golden years themselves: a time for exploration, growth, and embracing the beauty of the world around us. Like a caterpillar emerging from its cocoon, your retirement years are an opportunity to spread your wings and soar towards new horizons Set off on a camping or glamping expedition and let the serenity of nature rejuvenate your spirit. Remember, your golden years are an opportunity to embrace new experiences and reconnect with the world in meaningful ways.

Bucket List # 148

Participate in Outdoor Sports: Stay Active and Enjoy the Fresh Air

"Age is No Barrier. It's a Limitation you Put on your Mind." – Jackie Joyner-Kersee –

It's never too late to embrace a healthier, more active lifestyle. Participating in outdoor sports is a fantastic way to stay fit, enjoy the fresh air, and create lasting memories with friends and family. Whether you're a seasoned athlete or a complete beginner, there's an outdoor sport that's perfect for you.

First, consider the types of sports that most appeal to you. Are you a team player, or do you prefer individual pursuits? Do you enjoy high-energy activities, or would you rather engage in more leisurely pastimes? There's a wide range of options available, from tennis and golf to hiking and cycling. Don't be afraid to try something new or revisit a sport you once loved.

Once you've chosen a sport, it's important to start slow and build up your skills and stamina over time. Consult with your doctor before beginning any new exercise regimen, and invest in the proper equipment and attire to ensure your safety and comfort.

Consider joining a local sports club or group to meet like-minded individuals who share your passion. Not only will you benefit from the camaraderie and encouragement of your fellow enthusiasts, but you'll also have the opportunity to learn from their experience and expertise.

Moreover, embracing the challenges that outdoor sports present can help you develop resilience and problem-solving skills. As you navigate the ups and downs of your chosen activity, you'll learn valuable lessons about perseverance, adaptability, and personal growth. These qualities can be applied to other areas of your life, including your creative projects.

Outdoor sports can also be a fantastic way to bond with family and friends. Organize a friendly game of soccer, volleyball, or frisbee, and revel in the laughter and joy that comes from playing together. As you share these experiences, you'll create lasting memories and strengthen your relationships.

In conclusion, participating in outdoor sports is like a breath of fresh air, invigorating your body, mind, and spirit. Just as the wind propels a sailboat across the water, embracing outdoor sports can propel you toward a healthier, happier, and more fulfilling retirement. Get ready to embark on a thrilling new chapter of your life's adventure.

Bucket List # 149

Join a Nature Photography Club: Capture the Wonders of the Natural World

"Photography is a Love Affair with Life." – Burk Uzzle –

Nature photography is a delightful way to reignite your passion for life and rediscover the beauty of the world around you. By joining a nature photography club, you'll be able to connect with like-minded individuals who share your enthusiasm for capturing the wonders of the natural world.

The importance of joining a nature photography club lies in the camaraderie and inspiration you'll find among your fellow members. As you exchange tips, techniques, and stories, you'll gain valuable insights that can elevate your photography skills to new heights. Additionally, a club offers the opportunity to participate in group outings, workshops, and even photography contests, further enriching your experience.

Getting started is easy! First, do a little research to find a nature photography club in your area. Many clubs have websites or social media pages where you can learn more about their activities and membership requirements. Alternatively, you can inquire at your local community center or camera store for recommendations.

Once you've found a club that interests you, reach out to the organizers and express your interest in joining. Attend a meeting or event to get a feel for the group and see if it's a good fit for you. Remember to bring your camera, as you never know when inspiration will strike!

In conclusion, joining a nature photography club is like planting a seed in the fertile soil of your retirement years. As you nurture your passion for photography and connect with fellow enthusiasts, you'll watch the seed grow into a vibrant and beautiful garden, adding color and joy to your life. Go ahead and chase the light, for these are the best years of your life, and every moment is worth capturing.

Bucket List # 150

Volunteer at a Local Park or Nature Reserve: Contribute to Conservation Efforts

"In every walk with nature, one receives far more than he seeks." – John Muir –

Retirement is a time to give back to the world and make a lasting impact on the environment around us. Volunteering at a local park or nature reserve is a fantastic way to contribute to conservation efforts while immersing yourself in the beauty and tranquility of the great outdoors.

One of the many reasons to volunteer at a park or nature reserve is the chance to make a tangible difference in your community. By lending your time and talents, you help maintain these precious spaces, ensuring that future generations can enjoy them as well.

In addition, volunteering in nature offers a myriad of health benefits. Studies have shown that spending time in nature can reduce stress, improve mood, and increase overall well-being. Plus, participating in conservation efforts often involves physical activity, which is vital for maintaining good health in your golden years.

To get started, contact your local park or nature reserve and inquire about their volunteer opportunities. They may need help with tasks such as trail maintenance, tree planting, or guiding visitors. Don't be afraid to share your unique skills and interests, as many organizations are eager to find passionate volunteers who can contribute in diverse ways.

In conclusion, volunteering at a local park or nature reserve is a rewarding and fulfilling way to spend your retirement. By giving back to the environment and contributing to conservation efforts, you'll make a lasting impact on the world around you while staying active, learning new skills, and building meaningful connections.

Think of volunteering at a park or nature reserve as planting seeds for the future. Your efforts today will grow into a thriving, beautiful environment that will be cherished for years to come. This is your time to leave a lasting legacy and make the world a better place, one small act of kindness at a time. Embrace the opportunity to give back, and remember that your best years are still ahead.

Afterword

As we conclude this exhilarating journey, remember that "The Ultimate Retirement Bucket List" is just the beginning. Your golden years are a blank canvas, waiting for you to paint them with unforgettable memories and heartwarming experiences. Embrace your inner adventurer, cherish every moment, and continue to explore the limitless possibilities that retirement offers. The world is yours to discover, and the best is yet to come. Here's to a retirement filled with laughter, excitement, and unending adventure. Happy trails!